The World's Greatest
Snappy Comebacks

STORIES BEHIND THE FINEST WISECRACKS AND WISDOM FROM ANCIENT TIMES TO THE PRESENT DAY

Larry Lansburgh

The World's Greatest Snappy Comebacks/ Larry Lansburgh. —1st ed.

ISBN: 1533035423

ISBN 13: 9781533035424

Photos of Evelyn Waugh (p. 12) and Marc Connelly (p. 17) by Carl Van Vechten

Back cover: Photo of the author by Therese Hukill-DeRock

Contents

If you have ever thought of a witty response far too late,
or couldn't come up with one at all,
this book is dedicated to you.

CHAPTER 1

This Book

The Snappy Comebacks in this book include calm words spoken by a prisoner sentenced to death by hanging, biting comments from a ventriloquist's dummy who criticized his human for moving his lips, and a gracious response from a woman who was the world's leading arms dealer.

Snappy Comeback: a quick and witty response to an insult, a comment, a question, or a situation

Also among the 145 masters of the Snappy Comeback crowding these pages, are:

Writer Dorothy Parker, famous for a wit so scathing that people called her "the mistress of the verbal hand grenade."

The Duke of Wellington, famous for his defeat of Napoleon.

Zsa Zsa Gabor, famous for being well known.

The insult

This collection of wisecracks and wisdom is the result of an insult. Many years ago I had a summer job as an assistant carpenter, part of a crew remodeling a man's house. Our client came into the living room and looked at the rubble, the tangle of extension cords, and the drifts of dust a project like this always creates. He didn't say anything, but I had a feeling he'd had several beers too many.

Then he stared at me for a moment. He put his hands on his hips, and in a horribly condescending tone of voice said, "Well well well. Look who's wearing a brand-new tool belt."

His meaning was clear. Because my tool belt was new, he was implying I was inexperienced and therefore incompetent. I was neither.

But the unexpected attack rendered me speechless.

The Law of Invisible Opportunities

Over the years, I fumed about that insult, imagining how I might have responded to it. I could have replied by saying unflattering things about my client's ancestry. I might even have suggested he do something biologically impossible. Either of these responses would have gotten me fired on the spot. Even worse, they would not have been Snappy Comebacks because they would not have cleverly reflected his words back to him.

I recently imagined saying, "Well well well. Look who just drank up a twelve-pack of beer." Although qualifying as a Snappy Comeback, it probably would have gotten me fired too.

At first, of course, I couldn't see the opportunity hiding behind the insult. But as the opportunity slowly became visible, I began to collect Snappy Comebacks. I found wit and wisdom from people who lived a thousand years ago. I discovered zingers from people famous in their time, but almost unknown today. I remembered Snappy Comebacks delivered by family and friends. My collection became this book.

Are the Snappy Comebacks in this book really true?

The ones in my own life are true. For the others, the best answer is "Most are, some aren't, and sometimes we just don't know." As great Snappy Comebacks enter our folklore, the lines between fact and legend often blur. Sometimes it is impossible to know the exact wording or who said it first. To further complicate matters, some famous Snappy Comebacks become associated with people who years later deny they ever said it.

A story has it that the beautiful American dancer Isadora Duncan (1877–1927) asked George Bernard Shaw if he would consent to have a child with her. Shaw (1856–1950) wrote sixty plays and won a Nobel Prize in Literature. Duncan was supposed to have said, "You have the greatest brain in the world. I have the most beautiful body. Let us produce the perfect child."

According to legend, Shaw then responded: "But what if the child turned out to have my body and your brain?"

In 1926, Shaw wrote a letter in which he denied the conversation with Duncan.

Actor Cary Grant and bank robber Willie Sutton also denied producing the marvelous Snappy Comebacks attributed to them.

In 1986, the much-quoted Yogi Berra summed it up perfectly: "I really didn't say everything I said."

As my collection of Snappy Comebacks grew, I found a few that are clearly fictional, but too good to pass up. I couldn't resist sharing them with you, and I've labeled them as the marvelous fibs they are.

I've done my best to provide a historically accurate background for these Snappy Comebacks. When possible, I've listened to old recordings or looked at old movies to get the words exactly right. And I haven't trusted the Internet completely. Lots of web sites attribute quotations to the wrong people, so I've done a lot of crosschecking.

But this book is not a scholarly work. I haven't documented all the possible sources and variations of the Snappy Comebacks I found. A thicket of too many facts creates more shadow than light, making it difficult to master the art of the Snappy Comeback.

Can you master the Snappy Comeback?

Absolutely. It takes a bit of practice, but you've already taken the first step. You have this book in your hands. Your Snappy Comebacks have to reflect your opponents' words back to them. The key to that is the same key used to perform surgery, land an airplane, or handle explosives.

You have to pay attention.

This is a skill many people lack, but almost everyone can learn. Pay attention to your verbal opponents and reflect their words back to them. If your reply distorts things a bit, so much the better.

A fountain of Snappy Comebacks

Born into privilege, he struggled to earn a living by writing. A poor athlete with a weak body, he was a cavalry officer who participated in the British Army's last charge on horseback. He led England in her darkest hour, which he called her finest hour.

After saving his country, he was voted out of office.

CHAPTER 2

A Fountain of Snappy Comebacks

Winston Churchill (1874–1965) made more Snappy Comebacks than we can count. Every one was a gem. Churchill

was a mixture of opposites. He was charming and witty, but could also be difficult and abrasive. One day Lady Nancy Astor must have found him particularly grating.

"Winston," she said, "if you were my husband, I would put arsenic in your coffee."

"Nancy," he instantly replied, "if I were your husband, I would drink that coffee."

Churchill's early Snappy Comebacks

In 1897, Churchill was a young cavalry officer in the British Army. While on reconnaissance on the North West Frontier of India, his group was ambushed by Pashtun tribesmen. Bullets flew everywhere, but Churchill was not hit.

In 1898 he was in Sudan, part of the last cavalry charge of the British Army, and was at the center of intense fighting. Again, he was uninjured.

He loved the excitement. "Nothing in life is so exhilarating," he observed, "as to be shot at without result."

In 1899, just a month short of his twenty-fifth birthday, Churchill suffered a double disappointment. In his first run for Parliament, he lost the election. He also wanted to grow a fine Guardsman's mustache, but the result was nothing more than a sparse and pathetic collection of small hairs on his upper lip. Shortly after the election, he went to dinner, presumably still upset about these two defeats.

The woman seated next to him, a friend of his mother's, said she liked neither his politics nor his mustache.

"Madame," Churchill growled, "I see no earthly reason why you should come into contact with either."

In Parliament

Years later, one of his fellow Members of Parliament was making a speech so boring that Churchill fell asleep.

"Mr. Churchill," the MP said, "must you fall asleep while I'm speaking?"

"No," replied Churchill. "It's purely voluntary."

A person's sexual preference was not important to Churchill, but he could not resist a barb directed at a Labour Member of Parliament named Tom Driberg, a well-known seducer of handsome young men.

One day, Churchill learned from another Member of Parliament that Driberg was engaged to be married to a homely woman named Ena Mary Binfield.

Churchill's response: "Buggers can't be choosers."

The legend

Over his lifetime Churchill made so many Snappy Comebacks that his legend inevitably began to include mean-spirited remarks falsely attributed to him. For example:

> Woman: Mr. Churchill, you are drunk.
>
> Churchill: And you, madam, are ugly. But tomorrow I shall be sober.

Churchill never said this. It is an old joke, and a variation of it appears in the 1934 movie *It's a Gift* starring W.C. Fields.

Man: You're drunk!

Fields: Yeah, and you're crazy. And I'll be sober tomorrow and you'll be crazy for the rest of your life.

The declaration of war

On December 8, 1941 Prime Minister Churchill sent a personal letter to the Japanese ambassador in London saying England had declared war on Japan:

Sir,

On the evening of December 7th His Majesty's Government in the United Kingdom learned that Japanese forces without previous warning either in the form of a declaration of war or of an ultimatum with a conditional declaration of war had attempted a landing on the coast of Malaya and bombed Singapore and Hong Kong.

In view of these wanton acts of unprovoked aggression committed in flagrant violation of International Law and particularly of Article I of the Third Hague Convention relative to the opening of hostilities, to which both Japan and the United Kingdom are parties, His Majesty's Ambassador at Tokyo has been instructed to inform the Imperial Japanese Government in the name of His Majesty's Government in the United Kingdom that a state of war exists between our two countries.

I have the honour to be, with high consideration,

Sir,
Your obedient servant,
Winston S. Churchill

When a colleague criticized the letter for being too polite, especially at the end, Churchill replied, "When you have to kill a man, it costs nothing to be polite."

Churchill and Clement Attlee

Churchill and Attlee ran against each other for Prime Minister in 1945, and Attlee won. Churchill had just led his country to victory in World War II, and was shocked and devastated by the loss. Legend has it that Churchill bitterly remarked, "An empty taxi stopped in front of Parliament, and Clement Attlee got out."

Churchill said publicly that he would never make such a remark, and that Attlee was an honorable and gallant gentleman.

But another Snappy Comeback might just be true.

Unlike Churchill, Attlee wanted more government control over British life, including nationalization of public utilities and major industries. One day Attlee was standing at the trough urinal in the men's room of the House of Commons, when Churchill came in. Churchill stood at the other end of the trough as far away from Atlee as possible.

"Feeling standoffish today are we, Winston?" Attlee said.

"That's right. Every time you see something big, you want to nationalize it."

Randolph Churchill and Evelyn Waugh

Churchill's son, Randolph, did not inherit his father's wit. Randolph was an obnoxious bore. After a few drinks, he was also an obnoxious drunk. He was so unpleasant that his sister Mary said he "could pick a quarrel with a chair." Winston Churchill said he loved his son, but did not like him.

In 1944, writer Evelyn Waugh served with Randolph in a military mission to Yugoslavia. Randolph was a heavy smoker, and underwent a biopsy of a growth on his lung. The growth was removed and proved benign.

Serving with Randolph must have been difficult for Waugh.

When someone told Waugh about the results of the surgery, he said, "A typical triumph of modern science. To find the only part of Randolph that was not malignant and remove it."

The greatest Snappy Comeback of all time

He was called the ugliest man in England, but he had enormous self-confidence. He was a member of the establishment who enraged his peers by taking the side of the people. And he delivered a Snappy Comeback whose perfection is stunning even today, more than 200 years later.

CHAPTER 3

Classic Snappy Comebacks

John Wilkes (1727–1797) was an English political leader during the reign of George III. He angered the establishment

with his ideas on civil liberty and opposition to tyranny. Wilkes' support of the American colonists enraged John Montagu, 4th Earl of Sandwich, who said to him, "Wilkes, you will die either on the gallows, or of the pox."

"That, Your Lordship," Wilkes replied, "will depend upon whether I embrace your principles or your mistress."

In those days, "the pox" was an informal term for syphilis.

Nancy Astor

Nancy Astor (1879–1964) became the first woman to be seated in Parliament. The year was 1919.

One day Churchill said to her, "Having a woman in Parliament is like having one intrude on me in the bathroom."

Astor replied, "You're not handsome enough to have such fears."

On another occasion Churchill said, "I wonder what disguise I should wear to the masquerade ball."

Astor quickly responded, "Why don't you come sober?"

Mohandas Karamchand Gandhi

Gandhi's devotion to India's independence from England plus his unwavering commitment to *ahimsa*, non-violence, led many people to call him *Mahatma*, Great Soul. Someone once said to him, "You are a saint trying to be a politician."

"No," replied Gandhi. "I am a politician trying to be a saint."

James McNeill Whistler and Oscar Wilde

James McNeill Whistler (1834–1903) was a gifted painter with an outrageous personality. Short, with a slight build, piercing eyes, and a curling mustache, he was well known for his biting wit. The guests at an exhibition of his paintings in London included Oscar Wilde and Humphrey Ward, art critic of *The London Times*. Ward was expressing his opinions that one painting was good, another bad, and so on.

"My dear fellow," Whistler said to Ward, "you must never say this painting is good or that bad. Good and bad are not terms to be used by you. But you may say 'I like this' or 'I don't like that,' and you will be within your rights. Now, come and have a whiskey. You're sure to like that."

Wilde, delighted at Whistler's response, said, "I wish I had said that."

"You will, Oscar," said Whistler, "you will."

Oscar Wilde's life and wit were as much of an art form as his plays. When Wilde (1854-1900) arrived at a musical soiree in London, a woman approached him. She hoped he would be impressed by her niece, who was playing a Scottish reel on the piano.

"Do you like music, Mr. Wilde?" she fluttered.

Wilde, in kind and reassuring tones, cupped his ear in the direction of the piano and said, "No, but I like that."

Whistler and Frederic Leighton

Frederic Leighton (1830–1896) and Whistler, both great painters, had very different styles. Leighton's paintings were traditional, meticulous, and highly detailed. Whistler was a modernist who used free brushwork and deliberately flattened forms. One day the two were in conversation about their art.

"My dear Whistler," said Leighton, "you leave your paintings in such a sketchy, unfinished state. Why don't you ever finish them?"

"My dear Leighton," responded Whistler, "why do you ever begin yours?"

The Algonquin Round Table

The Algonquin Round Table was a group of well-known writers, wits, critics, and actors who met for lunch almost every day at New York's Algonquin Hotel from 1919 until about 1929. The luncheons were a feast of wisecracks, wordplay, and of course Snappy Comebacks.

Marc Connelly (1890–1980) wrote and directed plays, created lyrics, and acted. He received the Pulitzer Prize for Drama in 1930. During lunch at the Algonquin, a man passing the table stopped and patted Connelly's bald head. "Your head feels just like my wife's behind," the man said.

Connelly then felt his own head. "Why, so it does," he replied.

Humorist Robert Benchley was also a regular. As Benchley was leaving a restaurant, he asked a man in a fancy uniform to get him a taxi. The man gruffly replied that he was not a doorman, but an admiral in the United States Navy.

Benchley's response: "Then get me a battleship."

By far, the most scathing barbs came from Dorothy Parker (1893–1967).

Reviewing a play, Parker wrote that Katharine Hepburn's performance "ran the gamut of emotions from A to B."

About actress Marion Davies, Parker wrote, "She has two expressions: joy and indigestion."

In a review of a book, she wrote, "This is not a novel to be tossed aside lightly. It should be thrown with great force." She also said, "If all the girls who attended the Yale prom were laid end to end, I wouldn't be a bit surprised."

Parker always spoke in a soft voice, with a neutral expression. But her words dripped acid. At lunch one day, Alexander Woollcott recalled one of his book-signing gatherings. "What is so rare as a Woollcott first edition?" he bragged.

Parker immediately replied, "A second edition."

When she heard a friend had hurt her leg while in London, she said the woman must have injured herself sliding down a barrister.

Parker could also deliver a Snappy Comeback to herself, a rare feat. She had just returned from her honeymoon when *The New Yorker* editor Harold Ross asked why she was late with a book review. She replied, "I was too fucking busy. Or was it the other way around?"

At a Halloween party, someone made a comment about ducking for apples. "Change one letter," said Parker, "and it's the story of my life."

It is still hard to tell who were Parker's friends and who were not. She was equally venomous to all.

Claire Boothe was among the recipients of Parker's barbs. Boothe was enormously accomplished—a playwright, film scriptwriter, novelist, journalist, war reporter, and later US ambassador to Italy and Brazil. One day the two entered a hotel, perhaps the Algonquin. Boothe gestured Parker to go in before her, saying "Age before beauty." Parker obediently went in first, turned, and then said, "Pearls before swine."

At a dinner in composer Richard Rogers' home, Parker remained silent as other dinner guests happily criticized Claire Boothe, who was not there. Her only defender that evening was actress and novelist Ilka Chase, who said Boothe was always loyal to friends and kind to her inferiors. Without a pause or missing a bite of her dinner, Parker said, "And where does she find them?"

One day, someone at the Round Table asked Dorothy Parker to use the word "horticulture" in a sentence. She replied, "You may lead a horticulture, but you can't make her think."

In 1933, Dorothy Parker learned President Calvin Coolidge, a man of very few words and seemingly lacking in emotion, had died. She immediately asked, "How can they tell?"

Calvin Coolidge

But Silent Cal (1872–1933) had a dry Yankee wit. After an opera he had attended, someone asked him what he thought of the soprano's execution.

"I'm all for it," he replied.

At a dinner party in Washington, a woman sitting next to Coolidge told him she had bet she could get at least three words of conversation from him.

Without looking up from his dinner, he said, "You lose."

YouTube, Lloyd Bentsen, David Niven, and Anita Bryant

Sometimes it is hard to tell whether Snappy Comebacks are true or not because we lack proof. But now video and YouTube provide evidence.

In October 1988, vice-presidential candidates Senator Dan Quayle and Senator Lloyd Bentsen debated each other on television. Unfortunately for Quayle, the subject of his limited experience in public life came up. And Lloyd Bentsen came up with a double Snappy Comeback.

Quayle: I have as much experience in the Congress as Jack Kennedy did when he sought the presidency.

Bentsen: Senator, I served with Jack Kennedy. I knew Jack Kennedy. Jack Kennedy was a friend of mine. Senator, you're no Jack Kennedy.

Quayle: That was really uncalled for, Senator.

Bentsen: You're the one that was making the comparison, Senator.

During Bentsen's rehearsals for the debate, Congressman Dennis E. Eckart had told Bentsen that Quayle had previously compared himself to Kennedy. So Bentsen was ready, and in front of the cameras delivered a Snappy Comeback that instantly became part of political history. You can definitely create a Snappy Comeback in advance.

At the 1974 Academy Awards, actor David Niven was about to introduce Elizabeth Taylor, who would present the award for Best Picture. Back in the '70's, streaking—running naked through a public place—was a fad. Before Niven could introduce Taylor, a man named Robert Opel came out from behind the curtains and ran naked across the stage. As Opel streaked, the audience shrieked.

Niven, however, kept his cool. "Well, ladies and gentlemen," he said, "that was almost bound to happen. But isn't it fascinating to think that probably the only laugh that man will ever get in his life is by stripping off and showing his shortcomings."

The audience roared their approval of Niven's Snappy Comeback.

In 1977, beauty pageant winner and singer Anita Bryant, then in her thirties, was an outspoken opponent of homosexuality.

One day Bryant was giving an anti-gay press conference in Des Moines, Iowa when a gay rights activist ran up to her and pushed a pie into her face. In spite of the goo completely covering her face and dripping down her front, she managed a Snappy Comeback.

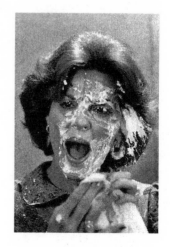

"At least it's a fruit pie," she said.

An early collector of Snappy Comebacks

He lived almost 2,000 years ago. Somehow, many of the Snappy Comebacks he recorded made it though the centuries and into the next chapter.

CHAPTER 4

Ancient Snappy Comebacks

Today we know him as Plutarch. He was born in southern Greece in 46 AD, and died about seventy-four years later. Many of the people he wrote about lived hundreds of years before he

was born, so the wisecracks and wisdom he recorded have reached us through a haze of oral history, legend, pure guesswork, a smattering of actual facts, and translations of translations of translations.

The legendary warriors of Sparta

Sometime between 900 and 800 BC lived a man who could have been a real person, or a legend, or most likely a combination. His name was Lycurgus, and he might have been the creator of ancient Sparta's harsh and effective military society. Most of Sparta's cities had no fortifications for a simple reason. No one could beat Spartans on the field of battle. According to Plutarch, someone said to Lycurgus that it would be a good idea to build a defensive wall around a particular city.

Lycurgus' response: "A city is well-fortified which has a wall of men instead of brick."

A visitor asked Anaxandridas II, the king of Sparta between 560 and 525 BC, why non-Spartan serfs worked in the fields, instead of Spartans themselves.

Anaxandridas said, "It was by not taking care of the fields, but of ourselves, that we acquired those fields."

Anaxander ruled Sparta between from about 640 BC to 615 BC. Someone asked him why the Spartans did not amass money in a public treasury.

He replied, "So that those made the guardians of the money do not become corrupt."

Polycratidas was one of a group of Spartans sent on a diplomatic mission to several Persian generals. The Persians asked him whether his group came in a private or a public capacity.

His answer: "If we succeed, public. If we fail, private."

Androcleidas was a Spartan who insisted on serving among the fighting man in spite of his crippled leg. Some of the fighters thought he should not serve because he could hardly walk, let alone run. Androcleidas' response used the typical logic of the warlike Spartans.

"With this leg, I can't run away," he said. "I'll stay where I am and fight the foe."

Archidamus, one of the kings of Sparta, was asked to settle a dispute between two men. He took them to a temple and made them swear to abide by the decision he would deliver. They gave their oaths to do this.

Archidamus then said, "My decision is that you are not to leave this sacred temple before you settle your differences."

Charillus was a king of Sparta in the 8th century BC. Someone asked him what he thought was the best form of government.

He replied, "That in which the greatest number of citizens are willing, without civil strife, to vie with one another in virtue."

Phillip II of Macedon (382–336 BC) had conquered almost all of Greece. The Spartans, who lived in southern Greece, were one of the few who resisted the formidable Macedonian army. In about 346 BC, the army approached a Spartan city. Phillip's emissary sent a written message to the Spartans. Although we don't have the exact wording today, the essence of the message was that, if the Spartans were defeated, Phillip's soldiers would destroy the city and kill every man, woman, and child.

Spartans were people of few words, noted for their laconic wit and for sticking to the point. Their response was a single word: **"If"**

Philip did not attack. Was his reason that the Spartans were such formidable warriors? Or was it their laconic response? We don't know.

There's even more to this story. Spartans called their homeland Lacedaemon (pronounced "La-kay-DIE-mon). From it, we get the word "laconic."

A 2,400-year-old Snappy Comeback

Alcibiades (about 450–404 BC) was an important Athenian statesman and general. He was also an orator who could hold his own in any conversation. One day he was in a debate with his uncle, Pericles, the greatest statesman, orator, and military leader of his time.

Pericles, wishing to disparage a point Alcibiades had just made, said, "When I was your age, I spoke just the way you are speaking now."

Alcibiades' response: "Oh, Pericles, if only I had known you when you were at your best."

The battle of Thermopylae

In 480 BC all of Greece knew that hordes of Persians were ready to invade, at a place called Thermopylae. The Persians numbered some 150,000. The defenders could field only about 7,000 men. Of these, the Spartans could send just 300 warriors, and each of the 300 knew he faced certain death.

However, being among the 300 was the highest honor a man could receive from the state of Sparta. Every Spartan man was a warrior, so not being chosen was a severe disappointment, even a dishonor.

A man called Paedaretus was not chosen, but he was strangely cheerful. His fellow soldiers knew him as a brave man, one who would willingly give his life for the state. They asked him why he was laughing.

"Because I congratulate the state of Sparta for having three hundred citizens who are better soldiers than even I."

At the battleground itself, a Spartan leader named Dienekes learned the Persians had literally thousands of archers who could shoot simultaneously. Someone told him that volleys of their arrows would blot out the sun.

"So much the better. We'll be able to fight in the shade."

The Old Testament

Even the Old Testament, a work not known for its humor, describes a Snappy Comeback by Ahab, the King of Israel.

Ben-Hadad I, king of Aram-Damascus, was preparing to attack and utterly destroy Samaria, Ahab's capital, and he sent Ahab a message.

Ben-Hadad's message: "May the gods strike me and even kill me if there remains enough dust from Samaria to provide even a handful for each of my soldiers."

Ahab's reply: "A warrior putting on his sword for battle should not boast like a warrior who has already won."

(*New Living Translation* I Kings 20:10-11)

Lesser-known gems

In the next chapter, a priest, a rabbi, and a minister....

Sounds like the beginning of a joke, doesn't it? In fact, the priest and the rabbi were friends. The minister, like anyone who takes a stand, made some enemies.

CHAPTER 5

Lesser-Known Gems
(a long time ago)

British Catholic Cardinal Herbert Vaughan was the Archbishop of Westminster from 1892 until his death in 1903. He was made a Cardinal in 1893. Rabbi Herman Adler became the Rabbi of London's Bayswater Synagogue in 1891. The minister was the Reverend Henry Ward Beecher, an American.

The Rabbi and the Cardinal

One day at lunch, the Cardinal jokingly asked his friend the Rabbi, "Now, Dr. Adler, when may I have the pleasure of helping you to some ham?"

Adler replied, "At Your Eminence's wedding."

The minister

Henry Ward Beecher (1813–1887) was a Congregationalist clergyman famous as an orator and an opponent of slavery. Like anyone who takes a stand on an issue, Beecher had both admirers and enemies.

One Sunday, he arrived at his church and found a note addressed to him. The note had just one word: "Fool!"

During his sermon, he told the congregation about the note. "I have known many an instance of a man writing a letter and forgetting to sign his name, but this is the only instance I have ever known of a man signing his name and forgetting to write the letter."

During the Civil War, Beecher traveled throughout the United States speaking against slavery and gathering support for President Lincoln. He said the Union would beat the Confederates in sixty days. It actually took four years. After the war, he traveled to England, where people were still sensitive about losing the Revolutionary War to the Americans.

During a speech in Manchester, a man asked, "Why didn't you beat the Confederates in sixty days, as you said you would?"

"Because we found we had Americans to fight," Beecher responded, "not Englishmen."

Sentenced to death by hanging

It would be difficult to produce a Snappy Comeback if you had just been sentenced to death, but an un-named English prisoner in the 17th Century did just that when he appeared before George Jeffreys, known as the hanging judge.

During the trial, Jeffreys (1645–1689) was in his usual vengeful mood. After he handed down the sentence, he stood, pointed his cane at the prisoner, and shouted, "There's a rogue at the end of my cane!"

Displaying an almost supernatural calm, the doomed man asked, "At which end, My Lord?"

Two Snappy Comebacks—one mean, one gracious

Noel Coward (1899–1973) was famous for his light comedies, and in his own words for having "a talent to amuse." But he must have had a mean streak as well.

One day he heard that a rather dim-witted impresario, a man he didn't like, had taken a pistol and blown his brains out.

"He must have been a marvelously good shot," Coward snapped.

When her father died in 1902, Bertha Krupp became the owner of Germany's, and the world's, largest producer of weapons. The company made cannons, tanks, bayonets, artillery shells— almost any steel implement that would kill people. The firm employed some 63,000 people. Each year Frau Krupp had a reception in her mansion for men who had worked in the firm for twenty-five and fifty years. During one reception, an old Krupp veteran wandered away from the crowd and strolled through the mansion opening humidors, and putting a few fine, expensive cigars into the breast pocket of his coat.

When he rejoined the group and made his farewell bow to his hostess, all the cigars fell out of his pocket.

Knowing full well the old fellow had filched the pile of cigars at her feet, Frau Krupp was graciousness itself. She smiled and said, *"Herr Schmidt, Sie müssen nie Ihre eigenen Zigarren bringen, wenn Sie uns besuchen kommen."* Herr Schmidt, you must never bring your own cigars when you come to visit us.

The Duke of Wellington and the French officers

In 1815 Arthur Wellesley, the First Duke of Wellington, defeated Napoleon near the village of Waterloo, in present-day Belgium. Wellington's brilliant tactics made the French retreat in panic.

Well after the battle, Wellington attended a reception in Vienna. When he entered the room, some French officers turned their backs on him. A woman apologized for their rudeness.

Wellington's response: "I have seen their backs before, madam."

Melville W. Fuller

Fuller (1833–1910) was the Chief Justice of the US Supreme Court between 1888 and 1910. During his term, he

administered the oath of office to five Presidents: Harrison, Cleveland, McKinley, Roosevelt, and Taft.

One day as he was presiding over a church conference, a man in the audience stood and began a tirade against universities and education. He said he thanked God no college had ever corrupted him.

Fuller interrupted the tirade. "Do I understand the speaker thanks God for his ignorance?" he asked.

"Well, yes, if you want to put it that way," the man answered.

"Then you have a great deal to be thankful for."

Mark Twain's written Snappy Comeback

With his flowing white hair and mustache, Mark Twain slightly resembled Fuller. One day, when Twain was walking down the street, a passerby stopped him, convinced the

humorist was the Chief Justice. The man handed him a pen and paper and asked for his autograph.

We can easily imagine the sparkle in Twain's eyes as he wrote:

It is delicious to be full, but it is heavenly to be Fuller.

I am cordially yours,

Melville W. Fuller.

Mark Twain the public speaker

Twain's writing was his springboard to a successful career as a public speaker. In the late 1890's, his address to the Savage Club in London was so well received that he was made an honorary member. He was told that in its long history the club had granted honorary membership to only three men, including the Prince of Wales.

"Well," Twain replied, "it must make the Prince feel mighty fine."

Back in the United States, just as Twain finished an after-dinner speech, a well-known lawyer stood up. "Doesn't it strike this company as unusual," the lawyer said, putting his hands in his trouser pockets, "that a professional humorist should be so funny?"

Twain instantly responded, "Doesn't it strike this company as unusual that a lawyer should have his hands in his **own** pockets?"

A $75,000,000 Snappy Comeback

Ambrose Bierce (1842–1914?) was a writer whose biting satire appeared in several newspapers, including William Randolph Hearst's *San Francisco Examiner*. In 1896, Hearst sent him to Washington to dig up some dirt on railroad baron Collis P. Huntington.

The US government had given Huntington's Union Pacific and Central Pacific railroad companies huge, low-interest loans to build the First Transcontinental Railroad. The loans totaled $75 million (worth about $2.2 billion today). That much was public knowledge. But Bierce discovered Huntington had secretly persuaded a friendly Congressman to introduce a bill that would forgive the debt.

34

Bierce's devastating articles revealed the scheme. He documented the facts, and as usual peppered his writing with insults including "the swine of the century." Public anger was intense. One day, Huntington must have had enough. He met Bierce on the steps of the Capitol and said he would pay the writer to stop writing. Bierce could name his price. Bierce made sure his Snappy Comeback appeared in newspaper headlines all over the country.

"My price," he said, "is seventy-five million dollars. If, when you are ready to pay, I happen to be out of town, you may hand it over to my friend, the Treasurer of the United States."

In a compromise, Congress approved an amendment to the bill calling for a sliding schedule of long-term payments over a period of eighty years. Neither side was pleased, but Hearst claimed a victory. And Bierce continued to insult Huntington.

Collis P. Huntington died in 1900. His remains rest in a grandiose mausoleum at the Woodlawn Cemetery, Bronx, New York. Eleven years later Bierce had the last word, in his most famous work, *The Devil's Dictionary*:

Mausoleum, *n.* The final and funniest folly of the rich.

Making a musician sweat

In 1917 pianist Leopold Godowsky and violinist Mischa Elman went to Carnegie Hall to hear a recital by a 16-year-old violinist giving his first performance in the United States.

The youngster was Jascha Heifetz, and his music went beyond brilliance. It was sublime.

During the intermission Elman, stunned by Heifetz's playing, wiped his perspiring brow and sighed, "It's awfully hot in here."

Godowski quickly replied, "Not for pianists."

Lesser-known gems (more recent)

The next chapter includes two Snappy Comebacks from military pilots. One of those responses might actually true. You'll also read about a man who called himself "The Greatest," even after a flight attendant gave a Snappy Comeback to his Snappy Comeback.

CHAPTER 6

Lesser-Known Gems (more recent)

A US Air Force legend

A story has it that at a pilot training base, quite a few student pilots were out flying solo in T-37's, twin-engine jet trainers.

One young lieutenant was practicing the loop, which requires the pilot to extend the speed brakes just after the top of the maneuver. Under the pilot's left hand are the throttles. The throttle for the right engine has two switches under the pilot's thumb. The top switch is for speed brakes and the lower switch keys the microphone. Every time this particular lieutenant did a loop, it got worse. Cursing at himself as he grabbed the throttles, he inadvertently pushed the microphone button.

Everyone in the air and on the ground was on the same frequency, so everyone heard the lieutenant's passionate string of curses. He ended by screaming, "Damn! I am a stupid son of a bitch."

Cursing, or even idle chatter, over the radio is strictly forbidden. The officer on the ground immediately keyed his own microphone and said, "Student pilot who made last transmission, identify yourself."

Realizing it was impossible for anyone to know who among all the solos in the air had cursed over the radio, the lieutenant once more keyed his microphone and calmly answered, "Sir, I may be a stupid son of a bitch, but I'm not **that** stupid."

Another Snappy Comeback on the radio

This one just might be true.

In the Persian Gulf, someone listening on the right radio frequency heard this conversation in English between Iranian air defense headquarters and an airplane near the Iraqi border.

Iranian air defense: Unknown aircraft, you are in Iranian airspace. Identify yourself.

Aircraft: This is a United States aircraft. I am in Iraqi airspace.

Iranian air defense: You are in Iranian airspace. If you do not depart our airspace, we will launch interceptor aircraft.

Aircraft: This is a United States Marine Corps FA-18 fighter. Send 'em up. I'll wait.

Iranian air defense: (silence)

A Snappy Comeback to Mohammad Ali's Snappy Comeback

The great heavyweight champ Muhammad Ali (1942–2016) was as famous for his boxing as he was for his ego. "I'm the greatest!" he often said. One day he boarded an airliner and settled into his seat, but didn't fasten his seat belt.

Flight attendant: Please fasten your seatbelt, sir.

Ali: Superman don't need no seat belt.

Flight attendant: Superman don't need no airplane either.

Obnoxious passengers, cool airline employees

A flight attendant's primary job is to manage and protect passengers in case of emergency. Fortunately, flight attendants can have a long career without an emergency. But when they encounter obnoxious passengers, great legends and stories come into being.

One story deals with a fussy woman who kept demanding small favors from a flight attendant. After a while, the woman became rude when she thought the flight attendant was not being sufficiently deferential.

According to the legend, the exasperated flight attendant told her, "Ma'am, I am here to save your ass—not kiss it."

On another flight, an obnoxious man spent the entire flight hitting on a female flight attendant. Every time she passed, he made inappropriate comments: asking for her phone number, wondering if she was busy that night, inviting her for drinks and dinner.

Toward the end of the flight, she was going down the aisle putting the passengers' litter into a plastic bag. The obnoxious guy had an empty soda can in his hand and asked her, "Are you picking up garbage?"

The flight attendant could not take it anymore.

"No, sir, I am not picking up garbage," she said in icy tones. "I am happily married."

On a flight across Canada, a flight attendant served a meal to a passenger in business class. The man took one bite of the meal and made a face.

"This meal isn't even fit for a pig," he whined.

"In that case, sir," replied the flight attendant, "we'll find you a meal that **is** fit for a pig."

Like flight attendants, gate agents sometimes have to deal with horrible passengers. At an airport in the Midwest, a crowded flight was canceled, and one single agent had to re-book a long line of passengers. Suddenly, an angry man cut to the front of the line, slapped his ticket down on the counter, and shouted, "I **have** to be on this flight and I **have** to be in first class!"

"Sir, I'll be happy to help you," replied the agent, "but I've got to help these people first."

Raising his voice even more, the man shouted, "Do you have any idea who I am?"

Naturally, everyone in line could hear him.

The agent smiled and picked up her public address microphone, knowing everyone in the terminal would now be able to hear her. "May I have your attention please? We have a passenger here who does not know who he is. If anyone can identify him, please come to gate 9."

That was her first Snappy Comeback, and everyone in line loved it. Another brilliant response came just seconds later.

The rude passenger glared at the agent and snarled, "Fuck you."

The agent just smiled and said, "I'm terribly sorry, sir, but you'll have to stand in line for that too."

Frank Zappa and Al Capp's wooden leg

This Snappy Comeback may not be true. Whether it is or not, it is too good to pass up.

In the 1960's, two great artists were on a television talk show—rock guitarist and composer Frank Zappa, and Al Capp, the cartoonist famous for creating *L'il Abner*, and for his contempt of hippies and rock music. A boyhood accident had caused Capp's leg to be amputated. He now used a wooden one.

On the show, Capp taunted Zappa about his long hair, asking him if he thought he was a girl.

Zappa is said to have replied, "You have a wooden leg. Does that make you a table?"

Man or woman?

Edna Ferber (1885–1968) was a Pulitzer Prize-winning novelist. Noël Coward (1899–1973) was an English playwright, director, actor, composer, and singer. Coward was not openly gay, but everyone knew his sexual preference. One day he encountered his friend Ferber, who was wearing a man's suit nicely tailored to her petite figure.

"You look almost like a man," said Coward.

"So do you," responded Ferber.

In the 1941 film *Never Give a Sucker an Even Break*, a lady asks W.C. Fields, "Are you really a man?"

"Well," Fields replies, "I've been called other things."

The setup

Every now and then it's possible to set someone up so you can deliver a Snappy Comeback. It's not really cheating. It's just spontaneity created by good planning. President Franklin D. Roosevelt and comedian Don Rickles created some fine setups.

In August 1943, President Roosevelt attended a highly secret conference in Quebec, where he, British Prime Minister Winston Churchill, and Canadian Prime Minister William Lyon Mackenzie King met to plan strategy for the war against Germany and Japan.

Then Roosevelt and Churchill returned to Washington. The President invited the Prime Minister to lunch at the White House, as well as Helen Rogers Reid, the publisher of the *New York Herald Tribune*. Roosevelt knew Reid was a fervent supporter of India's independence from England, and Churchill was adamant that India should remain part of the British Empire forever.

Roosevelt sat back at the lunch and waited for the fireworks between Churchill and Reid. He could not have known exactly how the conversation would go, but the setup was in place.

"Mr. Churchill," asked Reid, "what are you going to do about those wretched Indians?"

"Before we proceed further, Mrs. Reid, let us get one thing clear," Churchill replied. "Are we talking about the brown Indians of India, who have multiplied alarmingly under benevolent British rule? Or are we talking about the Red Indians in America, who, I understand, are almost extinct?"

Reid was speechless. Roosevelt roared with laughter. His setup had worked.

On Johnny Carson's show, Frank Sinatra told a story about the time Don Rickles set him up.

Before he was married, Rickles was having dinner with an attractive woman in a fancy restaurant. Frank Sinatra was at another table. Rickles told his date he knew Sinatra, but she didn't believe him. When she went to the powder room, Rickles walked over to Sinatra and said he really wanted to impress his date. Could Sinatra come by his table and say hello?

After Rickles' date came back to the table, Sinatra strolled over and said, "How are you, Don? Nice to see you."

Rickles looked up and scowled. With mock anger he shouted, "Can't you see I'm eating, Frank?"

Supreme confidence

Many people tell the story of a little girl who was making a drawing in class.

"What are you drawing?" asked the teacher.

"I'm making a picture of God," the girl answered.

"But no one knows what God looks like."

"They will in a minute."

Family, friends, and machines

The next chapter includes remarks from people I've observed in my own life, plus two Snappy Comebacks from machines. You'll also discover some calmly spoken words that instantly—and perfectly—avenged an insult.

CHAPTER 7

Family, Friends, and Machines

Snappy Comebacks can even come from machines. Several years ago, a friend of mine spent time with a family in Ecuador. When she got back to the US, she wanted to send a thank-you note in Spanish. She composed it in English, sent the text to a translation web site, and then asked me to check the computer's Spanish.

My friend ended her English draft with "Please give my love to the kids." The computer's translation was "*Por favor alimentar a mi amante a las jóvenes cabras.*"

I'm glad she asked me to check. In those days, translation software was far from perfect. The computer's Snappy Comeback had literally said, "Please to feed my lover to the young goats."

When we were kids, my brother, Brian, and our father went from our home in California to Nevada, where Pop was going to buy a horse. They stopped in the town of Ely to stretch their legs and get some gas. Taking advantage of being in Nevada, Pop began to lecture young Brian on the folly of gambling. To prove his point, he led Brian into the gas station store, where a row of slot machines waited for the suckers. Pop pulled a quarter out of his pocket. Saying it was illegal for a minor to gamble—and stupid for an adult—Pop put the quarter into the slot.

"Observe and learn," Pop said as he pulled the handle.

The three wheels turned to a marvelous accompaniment of mechanical clanking and whirring. When they stopped, they showed three bells, and the machine disgorged an avalanche of quarters.

That night, father and son had a fine dinner, paid for with several handfuls of coins.

Brian must have been immune to the slot machine's Snappy Comeback. Although he enjoyed his steak dinner, he never became a gambler.

Instant revenge

When he was in his twenties, Brian came up with a rare variation on the Snappy Comeback. Rather than responding to the person who had insulted him, he directed his response to someone else. The most clever words could not have produced a better result. I think even Winston Churchill would have been impressed.

In those days, Brian was a member of the United States Coast Guard. He was based just south of San Francisco as an Aviation Electrician's Mate Third Class, which gave him a great job—part of a team that saved lives.

He controlled the winch at the side door of a Sikorski HH52A helicopter. At the end of the winch cable was a metal basket especially designed to haul people out of the sea.

Coast Guard cutters did the same job, which led to competition between the airborne people and the sailors. The helicopters had the advantage. They could usually get to the rescue first. Brian writes:

"We'd be the heroes who plucked the victims from the water. The patrol boat, often a forty-footer, would be relegated to towing the wreckage or the half-sunken sailboat, to port. We Airdales would be showered with thanks and praise, while the poor schmucks in the boat would arrive in port to little or absolutely no celebration."

One day a man overturned his small sailboat in San Francisco Bay, and quickly became dangerously cold and tired. The helicopter, with Brian manning the rescue winch, arrived on the scene at the same time as a forty-foot cutter, in Coast Guard jargon a "forty-boat." The helicopter pilot tried to radio the cutter, but without result.

"No radio contact with the cutter," the pilot told Brian over the intercom. "Find out what he wants us to do."

Aboard the helicopter was a piece of equipment very useful in case of radio failure, a large chalkboard. Brian wrote "Need help?" in big letters on the chalkboard and showed it to the cutter crew as the helicopter hovered alongside.

In a situation like this, the pilot's job is to hover precisely, which he can only do by keeping his eyes on the horizon, not on what is happening below. The pilot depends on the guy in the door to speak into the intercom and give him directions about altitude and position such as "Right five feet" or "Down ten feet."

When the cutter's coxswain read Brian's sign, the old antagonism between airmen and seamen flared up. The man scowled and gave Brian the finger. Apparently, the cutter crew wanted the rescue.

Now came Brian's brilliant variation on a Snappy Comeback. He knew the pilot had not seen the coxswain's rude gesture. So ignoring the coxswain, Brian pressed his microphone button and calmly spoke to the pilot over the intercom.

"He wants us to pick up the guy in the water."

We'll have Brian finish the story:

> "Down we swooped and, with well-practiced competence, dropped the rescue basket alongside the victim. He scampered into it, we hoisted him into the helicopter and swooped off to the warmth of the Coast Guard Air Station. We left the forty-boat to drag the foundered sailboat back to the marina. As we departed, I could see the boat crew jumping up and down with anger. I smirked and solicitously covered our victim with a nice warm woolen blanket."

Pre-Columbian gold

While I was browsing through a jewelry shop in a small Northern California town, I noticed some old items seemingly made of solid gold. The saleslady breathlessly exclaimed, "All those are pre-Columbian gold!"

Quickly calculating that Columbus had come to the Western Hemisphere some 500 years before my visit to the store, and that the earth and all its elements were formed about 4½ billion years before Columbus was born, I replied, "All gold is pre-Columbian."

The saleslady was not amused, either by my irrefutable logic or my lame Snappy Comeback.

An "embarrassing" Snappy Comeback

When I was in college, I took some summer courses in Mexico, at the University of Veracruz. Several of us Americans were staying in a Mexican family's home near the campus. At dinner one evening, one of the American students spilled his glass of water on the table. He wanted to say, "Excuse me. I'm very embarrassed." But the house rule was Spanish only—no English. Honoring this sensible rule, he immediately said, "Perdónenme. Estoy muy embarazado."

I still give him high marks for thinking quickly in a foreign language, but his Snappy Comeback had one major flaw.

Embarazado, the masculine form, is never used. The word is always *embarazada*, the feminine form, for the very good reason that it means "pregnant."

The Snappy Comeback had two positive results. Our Mexican hosts absolutely howled with laughter. And my fellow student added a new word to his Spanish vocabulary.

A Snappy Comeback by my father

When my brother and I were in high school, we were having dinner with our parents in a restaurant. Pop sawed away at his tough steak without too much luck. When the waitress came by and asked how everything was, Pop pointed to his steak and replied, "I think they forgot to unsaddle it before they killed it."

I wonder if Pop lifted the Snappy Comeback from a 1941 movie, W.C. Fields' *Never Give a Sucker an Even Break.*

Waitress: And another thing. You're always squawkin' about somethin'. If it isn't the steak, it's somethin' else.

Fields: I didn't squawk about the steak, dear. I merely said I didn't see that old horse that used to be tethered outside here.

The setup

When Brian and I were kids in the 1950's, we had a dog named Tinker. One day Tinker had a severe case of dog-breath.

Several decades later we set our father up.

Brian: Pop, Larry and I feel bad about something we did when we were kids.

Pop: What was that?

Larry: Remember the day when Tinker had really bad breath? Well, Brian held him, and I brushed his teeth. Tinker really hated it.

Pop: Oh, don't worry, boys. You weren't being cruel, and I'm sure Tinker forgot all about it.

Larry: That's not what we feel bad about, Pop.

Pop: What do you feel bad about?

Brian: Pop, we used your toothbrush.

We hadn't really used Pop's toothbrush, but the setup got a fine laugh from our father.

The vegan and the pound of bacon

We all have a tendency to condemn people who do not share our views. Vegetarians can be militant about enforcing their politically correct opinions. Vegans are vegetarians amplified. We omnivores, of course, are mostly pretty mellow.

One day I was at the meat department in a local store. I told the guy behind the counter that I wanted a pound of bacon, and I asked if he could find some especially lean cuts. He showed me some.

"That's beautiful," I said.

A woman walking by overheard me. She stopped, put her hands on her hips, and asked, "How can you say that's beautiful? It's the carcass of a poor dead animal. I don't even eat eggs or dairy products. The planet would be better if everyone was a vegan."

"Oh, I'm a strict vegan myself," I replied.

"You are?" she said, confusion clouding her face as she stared at the package of bacon in my hands.

"Yes," I said, "but only between meals."

She walked away.

Kind words

My friend Jivan and I were building a wooden railing for a deck. We were taking great care to ensure that the pickets, the vertical pieces, were evenly spaced. As we put them in place, we were talking about a fellow we had worked with several times.

"That Bobby," I said, dredging up an old cliché, "is not exactly the brightest bulb on the Christmas tree."

I've never heard Jivan say an unkind word about anyone.

"Larry, let's put it this way," he said as he carefully measured the space between the previous picket and the one he was putting in. "It's just that the pickets in Bobby's brain are randomly spaced."

Where Snappy Comebacks flourish

One area of human endeavor is an especially fertile field in which Snappy Comebacks sprout and flourish. Here you will find ideal growing conditions—insane competition, enormous egos, an utter lack of shame, a biased press, and from time to time quick thinking. The field, of course, is politics.

CHAPTER 8

Political Snappy Comebacks

The second President of the United States, John Adams, had a low opinion of politicians.

"In my many years I have come to a conclusion that one useless man is a shame, two is a law firm, and three or more is a congress."

In *The Devil's Dictionary* (1911), Ambrose Bierce seemed to agree with President Adams.

Politics, *n.* A strife of interests masquerading as a contest of principles. The conduct of public affairs for private advantage.

Sir Ernest John Pickstone Benn (1875–1954) was a British publisher, writer and political publicist.

"Politics is the art of looking for trouble, finding it everywhere, diagnosing it incorrectly, and applying the wrong remedies."

Henry Clay, John Randolph, and their strange duel

Henry Clay and John Randolph were fierce political rivals. Clay was Secretary of State from 1825 to 1829. Randolph was a US Senator from Virginia at the time. One day the two men approached each other on a sidewalk so narrow that neither could pass unless the other yielded.

"I, sir," Randolph said, "refuse to step aside for a scoundrel."

We can easily imagine Clay stepping aside and with a flowing gesture of the arm saying, "I, sir, on the other hand always step aside for a scoundrel."

The conflict did not end there. In 1826 on the floor of the Senate, Randolph accused Secretary of State Clay of "crucifying the Constitution and cheating at cards." Clay then challenged Randolph to a duel. Every duel was a matter of honor, and the primitive state of medicine in those days ensured that even a minor wound could be fatal. In 1804, Vice President Aaron Burr wounded former Secretary of the Treasury Alexander Hamilton in a duel. Hamilton died several days later.

The duel between Clay and Randolph turned out to be the strangest duel in US history. It ended with no injuries and a Snappy Comeback.

Even with the primitive pistols of the day, Randolph was an excellent marksman. Although he enjoyed insulting Clay, he had no intention of hurting him. His plan was to shoot very high and miss Clay. Soon after the two met on the field of honor, Randolph's pistol went off accidentally, sending the bullet into the ground. Clay agreed the misfire was accidental and allowed the duel to proceed. But now Randolph was embarrassed about his misfire. So when the men had walked the agreed-upon number of steps and turned to shoot, Randolph did not fire high. He still purposely missed, but his shot came much closer than he had intended. The bullet put a hole in Clay's coat, but did not touch Clay. Clay also missed, then demanded another round.

On the second round, Clay missed, and again Randolph missed on purpose.

Their honor satisfied, the two men met at mid-field for a handshake.

Randolph said he owed Clay a new coat.

Clay's Snappy Comeback after his close brush with death: "I am glad the debt is no greater."

Eighty-eight years after Clay and Randolph shook hands, Ambrose Bierce was again right to the point in *The Devil's Dictionary*.

> **Duel**, *n*. A formal ceremony preliminary to the reconciliation of two enemies. Great skill is necessary to its satisfactory observance; if awkwardly performed the most unexpected and deplorable consequences sometimes ensue. A long time ago, a man lost his life in a duel.

Abraham Lincoln

In 1858, Lincoln and Stephen Douglas had a series of debates. During one of them, Douglas called Lincoln "two-faced."

Lincoln replied, "I leave it to my audience. If I had another face, do you think I would wear this one?"

Thomas Brackett Reed

Thomas Brackett Reed (1839–1902) was a Republican Congressman from Maine. Reed was Speaker of the US House of Representatives for two years, and then again for four years. During his time as Speaker of the House, he dramatically increased the power and influence of the position. Reed was a great speaker and a master of the Snappy Comeback.

Reed was so powerful that the Republicans were considering him for the party's nomination for President in 1896. Reed's comment: "They can do worse. And they probably will."

In fact, the Republicans did do worse. William McKinley was a mediocre President.

Reed disliked McKinley's successor, Theodore Roosevelt, whom he considered far too flamboyant and egotistical. "Mr. President," he said, "if there is one thing more than another for which I admire you, it is your original discovery of the Ten Commandments."

Reed had a powerful physical presence, more than six feet tall and nearly 300 pounds. But his large face was unremarkable. In 1891, the great portraitist John Singer Sargent tried to capture the formidable intelligence behind Reed's face.

When Sargent showed Reed the finished portrait, both men realized the painting did not truly capture its subject.

"Well," Reed said as he looked at the unsuccessful portrait, "I hope my enemies are satisfied."

On one occasion, a Democrat was debating a point Reed had made. Quoting Henry Clay, the Democrat said, "I would rather be right than be President."

As always, Reed was ready with a response. "The gentleman needn't worry," he said. "He will never be either."

Gerald Ford

More than sixty years later years later, when Gerald Ford was a Congressman from Michigan, he also made use of Clay's words. "Henry Clay said he would rather be right than be President. Now President Johnson has proved it really is a choice."

When he was President in 1974, Gerald Ford attended a Radio and Television Correspondents' Association dinner. Many people attending had been drinking heavily.

"At a time when funds for the defense budget may be cut," Ford said, "it's comforting to see so many of the big guns from your industry still getting loaded."

Agnes Macphail

Agnes Macphail (1890–1954) was active in progressive Canadian politics. She promoted her ideals through organizing,

legislation, and the columns she wrote for the *Globe and Mail* newspaper in Toronto. In 1921, she became the first woman elected to the Canadian House of Commons. Some of her colleagues welcomed her. Some did not. One of her opponents asked her, "Don't you wish you were a man?"

"No," she replied. "Don't you?"

Al Smith

Al Smith (1873–1944) was elected Governor of New York four times and was the Democratic US presidential candidate in 1928, running against Herbert Hoover. In 1932 he ran against Franklin Roosevelt. Both times he lost by a landslide.

During one of Smith's political rallies, he was interrupted by a heckler.

"Tell 'em what you know, Al. It won't take long."

"I'll tell 'em what we both know," Smith hollered back. "It won't take any longer."

Adlai Stevenson

Adlai Stevenson (1900–1965) was an American politician and diplomat. Famous for his eloquent public speaking and

towering intellect, he twice ran for President against Dwight D. Eisenhower, losing both times by a landslide. During one of these campaigns, a supporter said to him, "Every thinking person will be voting for you."

"That's not enough," Stevenson responded. "I need a majority."

A businessman and John F. Kennedy

A businessman visiting the Oval Office voiced his doubts about the economy because of the sagging stock market. Wishing to reassure him, Kennedy said, "If I weren't President, I'd buy stock myself."

"If you weren't President," replied the businessman," so would I."

Bill Moyers

One evening, when Bill Moyers was press secretary for President Lyndon Johnson, Moyers said grace at dinner. Johnson said he couldn't hear the benediction.

Moyers replied, "Mr. President, I wasn't speaking to you."

Pierre Trudeau

Canadian Prime Minister Pierre Trudeau (1919–2000) and President Richard Nixon did not like each other. In the 1970's, Nixon and some senior officials were talking about Trudeau. The President referred to the Prime Minister as a "clever son of a bitch" and an "asshole." The comments, caught by the White House recording system and later revealed publicly, came to Trudeau's attention.

"I've been called worse things by better people," he said.

New York Mayor Ed Koch

Reporter Andrew Kirtzman kept nagging Koch about a confusing statement His Honor had made.

Finally Koch said, "I can explain this for you. I can't comprehend it for you."

Ronald Reagan

In 1981, Reagan was seriously wounded in an attempted assassination and rushed to the hospital. Before he lost consciousness, it was clear he had not lost his sense of humor.

He said to the team of surgeons, "I hope you're all Republicans."

In 1984, Reagan ran again, against Walter Mondale. Reagan was the oldest presidential candidate in US history. When asked about his age in a debate with Mondale, he said, "I will not make age an issue of this campaign. I am not going to exploit, for political purposes, my opponent's youth and inexperience."

Mondale laughed. Reagan won the debate and the election.

Reagan loved to poke fun at himself, including his age.

"Just to show you how youthful I am," he said during a speech, "I intend to campaign in all thirteen states."

On another occasion, Reagan referred to his deputy chief of staff. "Mike Deaver in his book said I had a short attention span. Well, I was going to reply to that, but..." (pause). Oh, what the hell, let's move on to something else."

In a televised press conference, newsman Sam Donaldson asked, "Mr. President, in talking about the continuing recession tonight, you have blamed mistakes in the past, and you have blamed the Congress. Does any of the blame belong to you?"

"Yes," Reagan replied, "because for many years I was a Democrat."

Bill Clinton

In the 1992 Presidential race, Dan Quayle was George H. W. Bush's Vice-Presidential running mate.

Quayle said he was going to be a "pit bull" against Bill Clinton and Al Gore.

Clinton responded, "That's got every fire hydrant in America worried."

George W. Bush

In the summer of 2000, George W. Bush delivered a fine Snappy Comeback to members of the press traveling with him on his campaign airplane.

"I don't read half of what you write," Bush said to the reporters.

A reporter responded, "We don't listen to half of what you say."

"That's apparent in the other half of what I read," said Bush.

Barack Obama

In 2013, a South Korean immigrant without legal documentation shouted to Obama that the President should use the power of his office to stop deportation of illegal immigrants. Obama quickly reflected the man's words back to him, with elegant reasoning.

"If in fact I could solve all these problems without passing laws in Congress, then I would do so," Obama said. "But we're a nation of laws. That's part of our tradition. The easy way out is to yell and pretend that I can do something by violating our laws. What I'm proposing is the harder path, which is to use our democratic processes to achieve the same goal."

Another fertile field

Certain questions practically beg for answers that twist the meaning and make us laugh. The men and women in the next chapter provide those Snappy Comebacks.

CHAPTER 9

Questions and Answers

A question can be a beautiful setup for a Snappy Comeback. The unexpected shift of meaning in the answer gets the laughs.

When I was a teenager, my family had a houseguest named Bill. One evening my mother was expecting a phone call from a friend of hers named Hortense. My father was feeding the horses in the barn, and Bill was in the living room. The phone rang.

"Bill, will you get it?" my mother called from the kitchen.

Bill answered the phone.

"Is that Hortense?" asked Mom.

"No," replied Bill. "She seems quite calm to me."

Dolly Parton

Dolly Parton: singer, songwriter, actor, author, business executive, entrepreneur, and humanitarian. In addition, she is a master of the Snappy Comeback.

When asked if blonde jokes bothered her, Dolly replied, "I'm not offended by dumb blonde jokes because I'm not dumb. And also I'm not blonde."

People often ask her how long it takes to do her hair. "I don't know," she answers. "I'm never there."

Conversations with God

In 1995, the book *Conversations with God* came out. I went to my local bookstore to buy a copy. "Do you have *Conversations with God*?" I asked the woman behind the counter.

"Only after I've smoked a little pot," she answered.

Conversations with a waiter

When a waiter comes by with one of those enormous pepper grinders and asks if I want some fresh ground pepper, my response is usually "Yes, please." After he leaves, I might complain under my breath about a customer not being trusted to operate the thing, but I always miss the opportunity for a witty reply.

Then I discovered that the great humorist and radio and television writer Andy Rooney (1919–2011) had come up with the perfect Snappy Comeback.

"When those waiters ask me if I want some fresh ground pepper," Rooney said, "I ask if they have any aged pepper."

Conversations with a grocery clerk

On rare occasions restraint—what is not said—produces a flawless Snappy Comeback.

While I was paying for groceries in one of our local markets, an old lady approached. She was absolutely adorable, everybody's picture of the ideal great-grandmother. The clerk was a dignified man with a full head of white hair.

"Can you tell me where your nuts are?" she asked him.

With a matter-of-fact but friendly tone of voice, he instantly replied, "Aisle 23, next to the marshmallows."

She headed toward aisle 23. I looked at the clerk. He looked at me. Even though we two guys were now alone, I saw not even the hint of a smile. I found his respectful answer, and his unwillingness to go for the easy laugh with me, most impressive.

"Roy," I said, "you are a gentleman."

Mohandas K. Gandhi

Reporter: What do you think of Western Civilization?

Gandhi: I'm all for it.

Sarojini Naidu and Gandhi

The poet Sarojini Naidu (1879–1949) was the first woman to be governor of an Indian state.

She knew when Gandhi traveled by train, it was always third class, an important symbolic act. But he did not travel alone; a large entourage went with him.

The actual cost of his third-class travel, not to mention his other political activities, was enormous. Consequently, Gandhi was a constant fund-raiser. He especially depended on the large contributions of wealthy Indian businessmen.

When asked about Gandhi's ascetic way of life, Sarojini Naidu joked, "It costs a fortune to keep Gandhi living in poverty."

Groucho and marriage

Groucho Marx was having a conversation with his assistant, Erin Fleming.

"Don't you think a woman has a right to expect fidelity in marriage?" she asked him.

"Yes."

"What else do you think a woman ought to expect in marriage?"

"Infidelity."

Churchill's answers

In 1943, after his conference with President Roosevelt and Canadian Prime Minister King, Churchill visited Niagara Falls. Someone asked him what he thought of the falls. Churchill mentioned he had been there in 1900. "The principle seems the same. The water still keeps falling over."

A reporter asked Churchill what he thought were the most desirable qualifications for someone wishing to become a politician.

Churchill said, "It is the ability to foretell what is going to happen tomorrow, next week, next month, and next year. And to have the ability afterwards to explain why it didn't happen."

Calvin Coolidge

Back in the 1920's during a long rainy period, just to make conversation a Senator asked President Coolidge if the rain was ever going to stop.

"Well, it always has," he said.

Getting older

Here's a conversation I overheard in a local hardware store.

One fellow asked another if he'd noticed anything either physical or mental about getting older.

The second man replied, "I've recently noticed many disturbing things about getting older. I just can't remember what they are."

Marilyn Monroe in the nude

In 1952 Monroe posed in the nude for a calendar. When asked if she really had nothing on during the photo session, she replied, "I had the radio on."

A general's answer

Norman Schwarzkopf, Jr. (1934–2012) was a General in the US Army. In the early 1990's, he commanded the coalition forces in the Persian Gulf War. Years later, an interviewer asked him if he thought we should forgive the people who helped the terrorists behind the September 11, 2001 attacks on America.

Schwarzkopf replied, "I believe that forgiving them is God's function. **Our** job is to arrange the meeting."

A Navy SEAL's answer

When an interviewer learned of all the countries the SEAL had been sent to, she asked him if he'd had to learn several languages.

"Oh, no ma'am," he replied. "We don't go there to talk."

How not to get into the United States

Gilbert Harding (1907–1960) was an English journalist and radio and television personality. After a short time spent in Canada, Harding planned to go to New York. But first he had to get a visa at the American consulate in Toronto. This required filling out a very long form with scores of questions. As he worked on the form, his irritation grew. His patience was at an end when he reached a question asking, "Is it your intention to overthrow the government of the United States by force?"

Harding wrote his answer: "Sole purpose of visit."

Tattoos

You'll find lots of variations on this one.

Question: Do you have a tattoo?

Answer: No! Would you put a bumper sticker on a Ferrari?

Zsa Zsa Gabor

Someone asked Zsa Zsa, "How many husbands have you had?"

"Do you mean just the ones I was married to?"

A doctor asked Zsa Zsa "Have you had a checkup lately?"

"No," she replied, "but I've had a Hungarian or two."

John F. Kennedy

During World War II, Kennedy was the skipper of a PT boat in the South Pacific. One night a Japanese destroyer rammed his boat, cutting it in half. Two crewmembers died. The surviving

men swam to a small island three miles away. In spite of an injury to his back, Kennedy towed a badly burned crewman through the water to safety. Later, Kennedy and his executive officer, Ensign Leonard Thom, were awarded the Navy and Marine Corps Medal for heroism and the Purple Heart Medal for injuries.

When Kennedy was President, someone asked him how he became a war hero.

"It was involuntary," he replied. "They sank my boat."

Yogi Berra

"What time is it?" someone asked Berra.

"You mean right now?"

Oscar Wilde

Wilde once said it would be impossible to make a list of his hundred favorite books.

"Why?" someone asked.

"Because I have only written five."

A drawback of complaining to Oscar Wilde

Lewis Morris (1833–1907) was a Welsh academic and poet with sad eyes and a droopy mustache. Although Morris was knighted by Queen Victoria in 1895, to his extreme disappointment he narrowly missed being appointed Poet Laureate of England.

He complained bitterly about this to Oscar Wilde, saying, "There's a conspiracy against me, a conspiracy of silence; but what can one do? What should I do?"

"Join it," Wilde said.

Oscar Wilde in America

In 1882 Wilde came to America for a lecture tour. When he went through customs, he was asked if he had anything to declare.

"No. I have nothing to declare," he replied, "except my genius."

During the tour, he received a telegram from Griggsville, Illinois. "Will you lecture us on aesthetics?" the telegram asked.

Wilde's reply: "Begin by changing the name of your town."

A quiz show

These questions and Snappy Comeback answers come from the old television show "Hollywood Squares." I suspect the answers were scripted, but they got the laughs. Host Peter Marshall asked the questions.

Clifford Charles Arquette (1905–1974) "Charley Weaver"

Host: If you're going to make a parachute jump, at least how high should you be?

Charley: Three days of steady drinking should do it.

Host: Which of your five senses tends to diminish as you get older?

Charley: My sense of decency.

Host: According to Ann Landers, is there anything wrong with getting into the habit of kissing a lot of people?

Charley: It got me out of the army.

Host: When a couple have a baby, who is responsible for its sex?

Charley: I'll lend him the car. The rest is up to him.

Don Knotts (1924–2006)

Host: You've been having trouble going to sleep. Are you probably a man or a woman?

Don: That's what's been keeping me awake.

Rose Marie Mazetta (1923–)

Host: According to *Cosmopolitan*, if you meet a stranger at a party and you think he is attractive, is it okay to come out and ask him if he's married?

Rose Marie: No. Wait until morning.

Paul Lynde (1926–1982)

Host: Paul, why do Hell's Angels wear leather?

Paul: Because chiffon wrinkles too easily.

Host: It is considered in bad taste to discuss two subjects at nudist camps. One is politics. What is the other?

Paul: Tape measures.

George Gobel (1919–1991)

Host: Back in the old days, when Great Grandpa put horseradish on his head, what was he trying to do?

George: Get it in his mouth.

The dedicated bank robber

Willie Sutton (1901–1980) was a hard-working professional bank robber. Over roughly forty years, he stole an estimated two million dollars. He spent more than half his adult life in

prison, although he escaped three times. Sutton is still known for a classic answer to the question "Why do you rob banks?"

Our folklore says he replied, "Because that's where the money is."

Sutton's response, unfortunately, is fictitious. A reporter wanting to spice up a story probably invented the answer. Sutton later said that if someone had actually asked him why he robbed banks, he might well have said those same words because the answer is so obvious.

Willie Sutton's fictional Snappy Comeback had an unintended consequence. It led to a phenomenon called Sutton's Law, which is used to remind medical students doing a workup on a patient to look for the most likely diagnosis, rather than investigating every possibility.

So why did Willie Sutton rob banks? His real answer, while not a true Snappy Comeback, provides a fascinating glimpse into the thinking of a career criminal:

> "Because I enjoyed it. I loved it. I was more alive when I was inside a bank, robbing it, than at any other time in my life. I enjoyed everything about it so much that one or two weeks later I'd be out looking for the next job. But to me the money was the chips, that's all."

Delayed Snappy Comebacks?

A Snappy Comeback has to be snappy, right? Yes, most of the time. But sometimes a delay can be an art form unto itself.

CHAPTER 10

The Delayed Snappy Comeback

Sometimes circumstances dictate a delicious delay. Simply having to write a response creates a delay. On other occasions, the master of the delayed Snappy Comeback waits patiently for exactly the right moment to pounce.

Delayed Snappy Comebacks to a poem

William Norman Ewer (1885–1977) was a British journalist remembered today by a few historians as a spy for the Soviet Union during the 1920's. He is also remembered as the author of a little two-line poem. When he wrote the poem, it probably passed as wit, although today many people see it as anti-Semitic.

How odd of God
To choose the Jews.

Several people wrote delayed Snappy Comebacks to Ewer's poem. Unfortunately, we don't know the author of this one:

Not odd, you sod.
The Jews chose God.

The following response is attributed either to American war correspondent Cecil Brown (1907–1987) or to humorist Ogden Nash (1902–1971).

> But not so odd
> As those who choose
> A Jewish God
> Yet spurn the Jews

This gem comes from humorist and Yiddish scholar Leo Rosten (1908–1997).

Not odd of God.
Goyim annoy 'im.

(*Goyim*: Hebrew and Yiddish for non-Jews)

The shortest delayed Snappy Comeback

The shortest delayed Snappy Comeback in history came in 1862 from a company called Hurst & Blackett, the publisher of French novelist Victor Hugo (1802 –1885). Hugo was on vacation while his novel *Les Misérables* was being distributed. Naturally, he wondered how the book was being received. Hugo's telegraph to the publisher had only a single character:

?

Sales were excellent, so the reply was also a single character:

!

A doctor's response

Sir Morell Mackenzie (1837–1892) was a distinguished British physician who specialized in diseases of the throat. One day he received an urgent summons from James Macneil

Whistler, then at the peak of his fame for his brilliant paintings. Arriving at the artist's house, Mackenzie discovered that the patient was not Whistler, but his dog. Mackenzie was not amused, but he examined the animal's infected throat, wrote a prescription, and quickly left.

The next day, Whistler received an urgent summons from Mackenzie. Fearing bad news about his dog's throat infection, Whistler rushed to Mackenzie's house.

"So good of you to come, Mr. Whistler," said the doctor. "I wanted to see you about painting my door."

An exam at Yale

William Lyon Phelps (1865–1943) taught literature at Yale. One of his exams asked the students to discuss the "sprung

rhythm" technique used by poet Gerard Manley Hopkins. One student answered by writing, "Only God knows the answer to your question. Merry Christmas."

After Christmas, Phelps returned the paper with this note written on it.

"God gets an A. You get an F. Happy New Year."

Taking prisoners in World War II

In September 1944, during the Battle of Arnhem in Holland, John Frost was in command of about 740 British paratroopers holding the north end of the Arnhem Bridge. Opposing the British were some 16,000 German troops commanded by Field Marshall Walter Model.

The small British force not only refused to surrender, but surprised the Germans with continuous counterattacks. The battle continued until the British ran out of ammunition. John Frost was wounded and taken prisoner by the Germans.

This much is true.

But according to legend, at one point in the battle Model sent a messenger to the outnumbered British. Model's message said he wanted to "discuss terms of surrender." A while later Model read Frost's reply: "Sorry, we don't have the facilities to take you all prisoner."

Churchill and the preposition

Winston Churchill, a master of the English language, disliked verbosity. When he was Prime Minister, he read a report from a junior civil servant who had written a horribly

convoluted sentence in order to avoid ending the sentence with a preposition. Churchill sent the report back with a note at the bottom of the paper: "This is nonsense up with which I will not put."

Churchill and Shaw

George Bernard Shaw's most famous play, *Pygmalion*, opened in London on April 11, 1914. According to legend, Shaw sent Churchill a message.

"Am reserving two tickets for you for my premiere.

Come and bring a friend — if you have one."

We can imagine Churchill's thoughtful fuming as he held the message in his hand. "If you have one! Hmmm. That is what I shall reflect back to that scoundrel Shaw."

Churchill wrote back.

> "Impossible to be present for the first performance.
> Will attend the second — if there is one."

A telegram to Cary Grant

Back in the days when long-distance telephone calls were rare or even impossible, people sent telegrams when they needed to communicate quickly. Western Union charged by the word, and it was expensive. To save money, people left out unnecessary words. A telegram also contained no punctuation, so the word STOP indicated a period.

A publicity agent in Hollywood was writing a piece about actor Cary Grant, and he wanted to know Grant's age. Grant was in London, however, so the agent sent him a telegram:

HOW OLD CARY GRANT

Grant's delayed Snappy Comeback took the form of another telegram:

OLD CARY GRANT FINE STOP HOW YOU

Years later, a reporter asked Grant if the anecdote was true. "I wish I could say it was true," said Grant, "but it's not."

Great timing

Sometimes a pause makes a Snappy Comeback even better. The experts delay the thrust of the dagger until the victims work their way more deeply into the swamp.

At a party in Hollywood, Dorothy Parker listened to English actor Herbert Marshall (1890–1966), who, filled with his own importance, droned on and on about how busy he was. Again and again he bragged about his schedule, which he pronounced in the English way: "shed-yule." Parker waited for the perfect moment to attack.

Finally in her trademark soft and demure voice she said, "Herbert, you're full of skit."

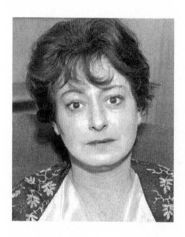

Parker attended another party given by film producer Arthur Hornblow and his wife, Leonora. Throughout the evening, Mrs. Hornblow kept talking about her theatrical career as a young woman. Time after time, she began a sentence by saying, "When I was on the stage...."

Parker let this go on for a while, and then commented, "Nonsense. In those days, boys played the women's parts."

Noël Coward pronounced his first name to rhyme with "bowl." At a party, actress Jean Harlow kept pronouncing it "No-EL."

Coward let this go on for a while, and then he said, "Miss Harlow, the 'e' in Noël is as silent as the 't' in Harlow."

Paul Dirac (1902–1984) was a Nobel Prize-winning English theoretical physicist who made fundamental contributions to the early development of both quantum mechanics and quantum electrodynamics. He was famously a man of very few words. After a lecture he gave at the University of Toronto, he asked if anyone had questions. An audience member said he had not understood part of a derivation.

Dirac did not reply.

His long silence became almost unbearable.

The audience squirmed.

Still Dirac did not speak.

Finally the moderator asked him if he wanted to answer the question.

Dirac said, "That was a statement, not a question."

More great timing

This one has been attributed to many people, including Wellington Koo. Even though it is not true, it is a classic delayed Snappy Comeback.

Koo (1887–1985), was a Chinese diplomat who earned his Ph.D. in international law and diplomacy at Columbia University. A distinguished statesman, he helped found both the League of Nations and the United Nations. After World War II, he was China's ambassador to the United States.

According to legend, Koo was the after-dinner speaker at a formal affair in Washington. Because there was no head table, he wound up sitting next to a woman who had no idea who he was. In those days, Asian faces were rare in Washington, and the woman must have assumed he spoke little or no English.

Trying to make conversation, she pointed to the bowl in front of Koo and said, "Likee soupee?"

Koo just smiled and nodded, and that was the end of their conversation.

After dinner, Koo delivered a learned and witty speech about international relations. His English went beyond being perfect. It was elegant. After he finished and as the applause died down, Koo returned to his table, smiled at the woman and said, "Likee speechee?"

A commencement speech at Princeton

Jeff Bezos, the founder of Amazon.com, spoke to the Princeton graduating class of 2010. He told a story about a road trip he took with his grandparents when he was about ten. His grandmother was smoking, and Bezos hated the smell of the cigarettes.

He tried using logic to convince his grandmother to quit smoking. Assuming that every puff took a few minutes from her life, he did the arithmetic. He then told her during the trip she had taken nine years off her life. He expected to be praised for his cleverness and math skills.

Instead, his grandmother burst into tears.

Bezos' grandfather stopped the car and signaled for Jeff to step outside. The grandfather then delivered some advice, a wise delayed Snappy Comeback.

"Jeff," he said gently, "one day you'll understand that it's harder to be kind than it is to be clever."

The US Navy versus Canada

The following dialog is clearly fictional. No naval crew in the world would make this mistake. In this version, some US warships were in the North Atlantic off the coast of Canada, when the fleet's radar detected something in the distance.

Navy Captain: (on the radio): Please divert your course 15 degrees to the north to avoid a collision.

Canadian voice: Recommend you divert **your** course 15 degrees to the south to avoid a collision.

Navy Captain: This is the Captain of a US Navy ship. I say again, divert your course.

Canadian voice: No. I say again, you divert **your** course.

Navy Captain: This is the aircraft carrier *USS Lincoln*, the second largest ship in the United States' Atlantic fleet. We are accompanied by three destroyers, three cruisers and numerous support vessels. I demand you change your course 15 degrees north, that's one five degrees north, or countermeasures will be undertaken to ensure the safety of this ship.

Canadian voice: This is a lighthouse. Your call.

Aircraft maintenance humor

The following delayed Snappy Comebacks could come from any commercial airline in the English-speaking world. When pilots discover something wrong with their aircraft, they fill out a form. These "squawks" then go to maintenance. Maintenance people reply with a note stating the actions taken. These bits show how a good delayed Snappy Comeback perfectly reflects the original comment.

Pilot: Left inside main tire almost needs replacement.
Maintenance: Almost replaced left inside main tire.

Pilot: Test flight OK, except auto-land very rough.
Maintenance: Auto-land not installed on this aircraft.

Pilot: Something loose in cockpit.
Maintenance: Something tightened in cockpit.

Pilot: Dead bugs on windshield.
Maintenance: Live bugs on back order.

Pilot: Autopilot in altitude-hold mode produces a 200 feet per minute descent.
Maintenance: Cannot reproduce problem on ground.

Pilot: Evidence of leak on right main landing gear.
Maintenance: Evidence removed.

Pilot: DME [distance measuring equipment] volume unbelievably loud.
Maintenance: DME volume set to more believable level.

Pilot: DME inoperable.
Maintenance: DME always inoperable in OFF mode.

Pilot: Friction locks cause throttle levers to stick.

Maintenance: That's what they're for.

Pilot: Suspected crack in windshield.

Maintenance: Suspect you're right.

Pilot: Number 3 engine missing.

Maintenance: Engine found on right wing after brief search.

Pilot: Aircraft handles funny.

Maintenance: Aircraft warned to straighten up, fly right, and be serious.

Pilot: Radar hums.

Maintenance: Reprogrammed radar with lyrics.

Pilot: Mouse in cockpit.

Maintenance: Cat installed.

Pilot: Noise coming from under instrument panel. Sounds like a midget pounding on something with a hammer.

Maintenance: Took hammer away from midget.

Ronald Reagan and the drunken master of ceremonies

In 1989, President Reagan attended a formal dinner in New York given by a conservative Catholic organization opposed to abortion. His speech to the group was crisp and articulate. But then the MC of the evening followed the President's speech with one of his own. The man had had too much to drink, and he slurred his words and rambled incoherently. He tried to praise Reagan as a defender of the rights of the unborn. Unfortunately, he confused the words "fetus" and "feces," saying all human beings begin life as "feces." The speaker even pointed out that Cardinal John O'Connor, sitting nearby and enormously embarrassed, had begun his life as a "fece," which he pronounced "fee-see." He then addressed Reagan.

"You, too, Mr. President—you were once a fece."

Aboard the presidential helicopter, Marine One, on his way back to Washington, Reagan commented to his aides, "Well, that's the first time I've flown to New York in formal attire to be told I was a piece of shit."

Actors

A former actor, Reagan could think on his feet and deliver great comments. But how clever are most actors, really? Are they only capable of speaking words written by other people? Listen to some of them ramble incoherently on talk shows, and you might think so.

However, some actors not only deliver lines well, they also come up with their own Snappy Comebacks.

CHAPTER 11

Actors
on Stage and Screen
(and off)

One of the greatest, and least humble, playwrights of our age, George Bernard Shaw, said, "I do not want actors and actresses to understand my plays. That is not necessary. If they will only pronounce the correct sounds I can guarantee the results."

Some actors, however, do more than pronounce the correct sounds. They write their own lines, and also produce some fine unscripted Snappy Comebacks.

Mae West

In 1926, West wrote, produced, directed, and starred in a play entitled *Sex*. The theater was soon raided, and West was

prosecuted on morals charges. She was sentenced to ten days in jail for "corrupting the morals of youth." But the publicity around her arrest quickly enhanced her career.

When questioned about all the efforts to censor her and impede her career, West replied, "I believe in censorship. I made a fortune out of it."

West (1893–1980) continued to write her own lines, even when she appeared in films written and produced by other people. She delivered her lines with a sexy tone of voice, and some of those lines made it past the censors, but just barely.

It's not the men in your life that count. It's the life in your men.

When I'm good, I'm very good. But when I'm bad I'm better.
From *I'm No Angel* (1933)

Hatcheck woman: Goodness, what beautiful diamonds!
West: Goodness had nothin' to do with it, dearie.
From *Night After Night* (1932)

A woman: Too many women follow the line of least resistance.
West: Yeah, but a good line is hard to resist.
From *Klondike Annie* (1936)

Man: Spring is the time for love.
West: What's the matter with the rest of the year?
Man: I wonder what kind of a woman you really are.
West: Too bad, but I can't give out samples.
From *My Little Chickadee* (1940)

The censors tried to repress West's overt sexuality, but of course had no objection to another star's image of blatant alcoholism and snarling hatred of dogs and children.

W.C. Fields

Born William Claude Dukenfield in 1880, W.C. Fields was famous as a hard drinking curmudgeon who despised children and animals. Parts of the private man matched the public image, and other parts did not. Like West, Fields wrote most of his own lines.

Question: Do you like children?

Fields: I do if they're properly cooked.

From *Tillie and Gus* (1933)

The 1934 film *The Old Fashioned Way* has a dinner table sequence in which the child actor Baby LeRoy throws custard into Fields' face, pulls his nose, and drops his pocket watch into a bowl of molasses. At first, Fields does a slow burn as he puts up with these assaults. But at the end of the sequence, Baby LeRoy is standing in a doorway, and Fields gives the kid a kick in the rear end. Audiences loved it.

At a dinner honoring Fields in 1939, a friend of his, the great American humorist Leo Rosten, stood up and spoke.

"The only thing I can say about W.C. Fields, whom I have admired since the day he advanced upon Baby LeRoy with an ice pick, is this: any man who hates dogs and babies can't be all bad."

In real life, Fields could tolerate dogs, and even had one of his own for a while. He was a kind man who loved his grandchildren and enjoyed entertaining the children of friends who came to his house. But Rosten's words (often incorrectly attributed to Fields) quickly entered our folklore and reinforced Fields' public persona.

On the other hand, Fields' image as a hard drinker was true.

For good reason, he never drank in his early vaudeville years. He was a juggler, one of the world's best, and he did not want to impair his amazing ability. "I could juggle anything in my day," he said. "Balls, cigar boxes, knives."

But by the time Fields had left the stage and was making films, he was drinking steadily. He wrote most of his own scripts, and made his heavy drinking part of his character.

Fields' niece: You know, Uncle Bill, I've been thinking. Why didn't you ever marry?

Fields: I was in love with a beautiful blonde once, dear. She drove me to drink. That's the one thing I'm indebted to her for.

from *Never Give a Sucker an Even Break* (1941)

Man: I have no sympathy for a man who is intoxicated all the time.

Fields: A man who's intoxicated all the time doesn't need sympathy.

Fields: Once, on a trek through Afghanistan, we lost our corkscrew, and were forced to live on food and water for several days.

From *My Little Chickadee* (1940)

Fields: Was I in here last night and did I spend a 20-dollar bill?

Bartender: Yeah.

Fields: Oh boy, what a load that is off my mind. I thought I'd lost it.

From *The Bank Dick* (1940)

But there was more to Fields' characters than alcohol. Fields as scoundrel and con man delighted audiences.

Cousin Zeb: Is this a game of chance?

Fields: Not the way I play it, no.

From *My Little Chickadee* (1940)

Man: Do you know anything about electricity?

Fields: My father occupied the chair of applied electricity at state prison.

From *The Big Broadcast of 1938*

Fields: You know, if anyone ever comes in here and gives you a $10 tip, scrutinize it carefully; there's a lot of counterfeit money going around.

Waitress: If I get any counterfeit nickels or pennies, I'll know where they came from.

From Never Give a Sucker an Even Break (1941)

Fields: My poor mother-in-law died three days ago. I'm attending her funeral this afternoon.

Secretary: Isn't that terrible, Mr. Wolfinger!

Fields: Yes, it's terrible. It's awful. Horrible tragedy.

Secretary: It must be hard to lose your mother-in-law.

Fields: Yes it is, very hard. It's almost impossible.

From Man on the Flying Trapeze (1935)

Fields' drinking finally led to a gastric hemorrhage, and he died in 1946. But his films still provide us with a seemingly endless number of Snappy Comebacks and wisecracks.

Hangman: Have you any last wish?

Fields: Yes, I'd like to see Paris before I die. (pause) Philadelphia will do.

From My Little Chickadee

According to the Fields myth, in his final days, although he was never religious, he was reading the Bible. When asked why, he responded, "I'm looking for loopholes."

Grouco Marx

Groucho (1890–1977) was a quick-witted comedian whose career started on the vaudeville stage with his brothers and ended on television with his popular quiz show, *You Bet Your Life*. His trademark appearance—stooped posture while he walked, horn-rimmed glasses, cigar, and thick greasepaint mustache and eyebrows—resulted in the famous novelty disguise known as Groucho Glasses.

Insults were a big part of Marx Brothers films. In a battle scene in *Duck Soup* (1933), Groucho looks at Mrs. Gloria Teasdale (played by Margaret Dumont) and says to the other Marx brothers, "Remember, you're fighting for this woman's honor, which is probably more than she ever did."

Groucho's insults were part of his personal life as well. He publicly insulted most of his friends, and as with comedian Don Rickles a generation later, it became an honor to receive those jibes.

One evening in a restaurant a man approached Groucho and said, "My wife is a big fan of yours, and is dying to be insulted by you. Would you please insult her?"

Groucho looked at the woman, and then turned his attention back to the husband. "Sir, I'm surprised at you," he said. "With a wife like that, you ought to be able to come up with your own insults."

Someone once said to Groucho, "You probably don't remember me."

"I never forget a face," replied Groucho, "but in your case I'll be glad to make an exception."

Later in life, Groucho sometimes mentioned that he could no longer give anyone a true insult because the person being insulted would laugh, feeling flattered to be the recipient of one of Groucho's jokes.

During his final days in the Cedars Sinai Medical Center in Los Angeles, a nurse came to Groucho's bed with a thermometer and told him she wanted to see if he had a temperature.

Even in his feeble state he managed a Snappy Comeback: "Don't be silly—everybody has a temperature."

The tyrant

Cecil B. DeMille produced and directed films of an epic scale such as *The Greatest Show on Earth* (1952) and *The Ten Commandments* (1956), movies that literally had casts of

thousands. He was one of the first film directors to become a celebrity in his own right. And he was a tyrant who demanded complete obedience.

During the filming of *The Sign of the Cross* (1932), DeMille held a microphone and was issuing orders to a huge number of extras—people playing Christians, Romans, and gladiators. Then he spotted one young woman who was whispering to another extra.

Furious, DeMille shouted, "Wouldn't you like to share your thoughts with the rest of us?"

The young woman, embarrassed, shook her head.

DeMille insisted she come to the center of the arena, where he was standing. She did, and he handed her the microphone. "Tell us what you were saying," he commanded.

The woman took the microphone, squared her shoulders, and addressed the hundreds of people in front of her. "When is this bald-headed old bastard going to call lunch?"

In those days, women did not use such language. No one spoke, terrified at what was surely going to happen next.

But DeMille must have admired her boldness. He threw back his head and laughed. Then he took the microphone back and spoke to the cast.

"This bald-headed old bastard is going to let you go to lunch this minute. Lunch!"

More movies and plays, plus a radio show

The Ruling Class, a play written in 1968 by Peter Barnes is a comedy focusing on the Earl of Gurney and the attempts to cure him of insanity.

> Claire: How do you know you're God?
>
> Earl of Gurney: Simple. When I pray to Him, I find I'm talking to myself.

Brendan Behan (1923–1964) was an Irish playwright who was also a poet and novelist. Behan had a severe drinking problem, but he described himself as "a drinker with a writing problem." His play *The Hostage* has this bit of dialogue.

> Pat: He was an Anglo-Irishman.
>
> Meg: In the blessed name of God, what's that?
>
> Pat: A Protestant with a horse.

In the 1996 film *Evita*, Madonna plays Eva Perón. The real Eva Perón, born in 1919, was not just the wife of Argentine President Juan Perón. She was a powerful social and political force in her own right. Just before her death from cancer at age

33, the Congress of Argentina gave her the title "Spiritual Leader of the Nation."

In the film, written by Alan Parker and Oliver Stone, John Gower plays the fictional Prince Fuspoli, a retired admiral. In the film as in real life, some people suspected that Eva, a former model, tango singer, actress and radio personality, had slept her way to the top.

> Eva Perón: Did you hear that? They called me a whore! They actually called me a whore!
>
> Prince Fuspoli: Signora Perón, it's an easy mistake. I haven't been to sea for years, but they still call me admiral.

In the film *Casablanca*, Humphrey Bogart is Rick Blaine, and Peter Lorre has the role of Signor Ugarte. This Snappy Comeback comes as the two are playing chess.

> Ugarte: You despise me, don't you?
>
> Rick: If I gave you any thought, I probably would.

Oscar Wilde's play *The Importance of Being Earnest* has been delighting audiences since 1895.

> Lady Bracknell: Are your parents living?
>
> Jack: I have lost both my parents.

Lady Bracknell: To lose one parent, Mr. Worthing, may be regarded as a misfortune; to lose both looks like carelessness.

***

Jack: I am in love with Gwendolen. I have come up to town expressly to propose to her.

Algernon: I thought you had come up for pleasure. I call that business.

Jack: How utterly unromantic you are!

Algernon: I really don't see anything romantic in proposing. It's very romantic to be in love. But there is nothing romantic about a definite proposal. Why, one may be accepted. One usually is, I believe. Then the excitement is all over. The very essence of romance is uncertainty. If ever I get married, I'll certainly try to forget the fact.

Jack: I have no doubt about that, dear Algy. The Divorce Court was specially invented for people whose memories are so curiously constituted.

***

Cecily: I don't believe him. But that does not affect the wonderful beauty of his answer.

Gwendolen: True. In matters of grave importance, style, not sincerity, is the vital thing.

After a performance of one of his plays, Oscar Wilde went on stage to take a bow and enjoy the applause. Some people threw flowers onto the stage, but one man threw a rotten cabbage at the playwright.

Wilde picked up the stinking cabbage, sniffed it, and said in the kindest tones, "Thank you, my friend. Every time I smell it, I shall be reminded of you."

Comedian Jack Benny (1894–1974) worked the complete spectrum of show business—vaudeville in the early years of the 20th Century, radio from the 1930's to the 1950's, television and movies from 1949 to 1965.

Benny's comic persona was a penny-pinching miser. His timing was flawless. He could get tremendous laughs simply with a pause.

In his radio show of March 28, 1948, a skit portrayed Benny being accosted by a mugger.

> Mugger: Don't make a move, this is a stickup. Now, come on. Your money or your life.
>
> (A very long pause; audience laughter)
>
> Mugger: Look, bud! I said your money or your life!
>
> Benny: I'm thinking it over!

Actors off-stage and off-camera

Some people thought that early in his career, actor Burt Reynolds looked like Marlon Brando. In fact, Reynolds did play an actor based on Brando in an episode of the television series *The Twilight Zone*. When Brando finally met Reynolds, the older actor grew abusive, accusing Reynolds on capitalizing on the resemblance.

Reynolds courteously replied that he refused to have surgery to change his face. "But," he added (and here came the Snappy Comeback), "I promise not to get fat."

The great Egyptian actor Omar Sharif (1932–2015) came to the world's attention with his appearance in *Lawrence of Arabia*. The movie *Doctor Zhivago* made him an international star. Actor and writer Aasif Mandvi recalled the time he was working as a waiter and had the chance to serve Sharif.

"*Doctor Zhivago* changed my life," Mandvi said to the actor.

Sharif leaned forward and smiled. "Really? Mine too."

In her prime, Sarah Bernhardt (1844–1923) was the grande dame of the European theater. According to one story, a younger actress approached her to ask for an autograph just before Bernhardt was to go on stage. Noticing Bernhardt's hand shaking, the young actress said she never got nervous before a performance. She asked Bernhardt how such an accomplished actress could be so nervous.

Bernhardt replied, "You will get nervous too—when you learn how to act."

Tallulah Bankhead (1902–1968) was a brilliant American actress of the stage and screen. She was also famous for a sharp wit and many, many affairs.

One day she encountered a former lover, whom she hadn't seen in years.

"I thought I told you to wait in the car," she said.

After her breakup with Tom Cruise, who was several inches shorter, Nicole Kidman appeared on David Letterman's show and was asked how she was doing. "Well, I can wear heels now," she replied.

Ventriloquists

Being a ventriloquist is one of the most difficult gigs in show business. These people need excellent visuals—dummies that can roll their eyes, look around, move their arms, even change expressions. Ventriloquists have to be both actors and stand-up comics. They need superb timing, material that makes people laugh, and the ability to think on their feet. And, of course, they do all of this without moving their lips.

One ventriloquist had a dummy as famous as any movie star. This man's timing and material were superb. His dummy's appearance and movements were great. His one minor flaw was that now and then you could see his lips moving.

But he did something no other ventriloquist did before, or has done since.

CHAPTER 12

A Dummy's Snappy Comebacks

Edgar Bergen was the only ventriloquist who had his own radio show. In radio the choice is always simple—great spoken material or failure. Starting in 1937, Bergen was on the air for nineteen years.

Bergen had three dummies. Mortimer Snerd was a dim-witted bumpkin. Effie Klinker was a man-crazy old lady. But the star was Charlie McCarthy.

In those days, Charlie was as famous as any movie star— and had a stronger personality than most. You never knew what outrageous thing he would say. Charlie was boastful and irreverent. He often produced sly double meanings no censor would ever allow a real human to say. Even today, when we see an old video or listen to an even older audio recording, it's easy to believe the kindly Bergen and the outrageous McCarthy were two different people—especially when Charlie pointed out that Bergen was moving his lips while he, Charlie, was talking.

This contrast, this dynamic, was Edgar Bergen's creation. It made him a wealthy man, and it made the acid-tongued Charlie McCarthy a household name

A visit to Edgar Bergen's house

Bergen (1903–1978) was a friend of my parents, and he even had a supporting role in a movie my father made in 1953. I was a little kid in the early 1950's, but I remember visiting Bergen's beautiful Spanish-style house on a hill in the Los Angeles area. Bergen met us at the front door. As he and I shook hands, I had the impression of an easy-going man—exactly his stage persona.

We went into the house, turned to the left, and went down a short hall. Another left from the hall, and we were in the star's room. Almost everyone in the country would have loved to be where I was. The room actually contained several Charlies. If you're a star, you need a stand-in, maybe a stuntman, and in Charlie's case a few spare parts. The room also contained a lot of small, flashy clothes.

My childhood memories of the details are a bit hazy, but my recent research has revealed the contents of Charlie's wardrobe. In addition to two formal outfits, he had several monocles and starched linen shirts, lots of hats (size 3½), including several top hats and two berets. Charlie could dress up as a cowboy, jockey, French Foreign legionnaire, gypsy, and Sherlock Holmes. In the 1930's, Bergen's costume and laundry bill was some $1,000 a year, a huge amount of money at the time.

Bergen insured his star for $10,000 against damage or theft. Of course, you don't need a dummy and costumes on a radio show. Bergen was so popular that he could have shown up for his show with nothing but his voice. But he had Charlie, immaculate in top hat and tails on his lap, for the very good reason that he had a live audience.

Cub Scouts in the audience

Edgar Bergen and Charlie McCarthy filled an auditorium every week, and the audiences loved them. One of those audiences included my Cub Scout den. After the show, my father led us backstage and took a picture. I'm third from the left.

Edgar Bergen and W.C. Fields

Many years before our backstage visit, one of the stars on Bergen's radio show, the *Chase and Sanborn Hour*, was the great W.C. Fields. Few performers were a match for Fields, but

Bergen definitely was. He had created a strong, sharp-witted character in Charlie, and he and his writers were highly skilled in the art of the Snappy Comeback. Charlie joked that Fields was a drunk with a bulbous nose. Fields responded with comments about Charlie being made of wood. These back-and-forth Snappy Comebacks created a classic feud.

Fields: Well, if it isn't Charlie McCarthy, the woodpecker's pinup boy.

Charlie: Well, if it isn't W.C. Fields, the man who keeps Seagram's in business.

Fields: I love children. I can remember when, with my own little unsteady legs, I toddled from room to room.

Charlie: When was that? Last night?

Fields: Quiet, Wormwood, or I'll whittle you into a Venetian blind.

Charlie: Ooh, that makes me shutter!

Fields: Tell me, Charles, is it true that your father was a gate-leg table?

Charlie: If it is, your father was under it.

Fields: Why, you stunted spruce, I'll throw a Japanese beetle on you.

Charlie: Why, you barfly you, I'll stick a wick in your mouth, and use you for an alcohol lamp.

Fields: Step out of the sun, Charles. You may come unglued.

Charlie: Mind if I stand in the shade of your nose?

Charlie (to the audience): Pink elephants take aspirin to get rid of W. C. Fields.

In a different *Chase and Sanborn Hour*, a skit has Fields playing golf with Charlie as his caddy. Unsure about his score, Fields turns to Charlie.

> Fields: How do I stand?
>
> Charlie: I often wonder.

Charlie McCarthy and women

Charlie was obsessed with women, and many of his comments had sexual double-meanings only a character made of wood could deliver. If his comments had come from a real person in those straight-laced days, they would have been censored.

On one show, the guest star was Dale Evans, "Queen of the West" and wife of the "King of the Cowboys," Roy Rogers.

> Charlie: May I have a kiss good-bye?
>
> Evans: Well, I can't see any harm in that.
>
> Charlie: Oh. I wish you could. A harmless kiss doesn't sound very thrilling.

No one objected to the dialog with Dale Evans. Mae West, on the other hand, brought the conversation with Charlie much closer to the line. Here's part of a conversation between the two on December 12, 1937.

> West: Charlie, are these your keys?
>
> Charlie: Did I leave them in the car?
>
> West: No. You left them in my apartment.
>
> Bergen: Charlie, where did you leave those keys?
>
> Charlie: (stuttering)
>
> West: He left them on my dresser. So what? Charlie, why don't you walk out on Bergen? What's holding you?
>
> Charlie: He is. (laughter) You better tell him, Mae.

West: If you want to know, he did come up to see me.

Bergen: Oh, he did? And what was he doing up there?

West: Well, Charlie came up and I showed him my etchings. (pause, laughter from audience) And he showed me his stamp collection.

Charlie: There you have it, Bergen, there you have it.

Bergen: So that's all there was to it, just etchings and a stamp collection.

Charlie (to West): He's so naive. (big audience reaction)

West: I thought we were going to have a nice long talk Tuesday night at my apartment. Where did you go when the doorbell rang?

Charlie: Well, I tried to hide in your clothes closet, but two guys kicked me out.

West: Why don't you come home with me now, honey. I'll let you play in my woodpile. So Good Time Charlie's going to play hard to get. You can't kid me. You're afraid of women.

Charlie: Not so loud, Mae, not so loud. All my girlfriends are listening.

West: Oh, yeah? You're all wood and a yard long.

Charlie: Yeah.

West: You weren't so nervous and backward when you came up to see me at my apartment. In fact, you didn't need any encouragement to kiss me.

Charlie: Did I do that?

West: Why, you certainly did. I got marks to prove it. An' splinters, too.

The Mae West incident

In a skit later in the same show, West played Eve to announcer Don Ameche's Adam. But she did not completely follow the script. She invented many of her lines on the spot— using her usual sexy delivery. That was her downfall.

116

One line she improvised was to the serpent in the Garden of Eden.

"I feel like doin' a big apple," she said.

These words, plus her sultry delivery, raised a few eyebrows. But then the serpent got stuck in a picket fence when it was trying to reach the forbidden fruit. West's delivery sounded like a woman having an orgasm.

"There! There! Now you're through!"

The live audience enjoyed the skit. Edgar Bergen was shocked. The sponsor, the censors, and every radio network blacklisted West. She was banned from radio for fifteen years.

It's important to remember that any Snappy Comeback can backfire—even if you're talking to a snake trying to get through a picket fence.

The photograph

As we prepared to leave the Bergen house, Pop wanted to take a picture of me with Bergen's daughter. Candy and I were assigned to sit on her little hobbyhorse.

As you can see, there wasn't much chemistry between us. It

was more like physics. The sun was in my eyes, and gravity made Candy slip off the back of the horse.

After co-starring with me in front of Pop's old Rolleiflex still camera, she went on to far better things. Among many other honors, Candace Bergen received an Academy Award nomination for her supporting role in the film *Starting Over*. She also won five Emmy Awards and two Golden Globe Awards for her ten seasons starring in the TV sitcom *Murphy Brown*. On the show, she delivered plenty of Snappy Comebacks.

Murphy Brown

In the sitcom, Candice Bergen plays Murphy Brown, a famous news anchor and investigative reporter. In an episode called "The Morning Show," written by Kathryn Baker, Murphy is assigned to co-host the morning show, but hates the job.

> Murphy: As if I really wanted to get up at 3:00 AM to interview some flash-in-the-pan starlet or health-food nut for the sole purpose of entertaining late-to-work slackards or the chronically unemployed and hooking them on a daylong spree of soap operas.

In the episode "From Here to Jerusalem," written by Hayes Jackson, Murphy has been dating a much younger man. Her colleagues are concerned. Frank Fontana, the investigative reporter played by Joe Regalbuto, says the young man is not her type.

> Murphy: You mean the young type?
>
> Frank: Yeah. That's it.
>
> Murphy: When did that ever stop you Frank? I've seen you squire around Junior Achievement winners.
>
> Frank: It's different. It's different.
>
> Murphy: Different? This is the oldest double standard in the book. When Picasso was seventy he was dating twenty-five-year-olds, and men all around the world applauded. But if Margaret Thatcher showed up with a twenty-five-year-old, the townspeople would chase after her with torches of fire.

Snappy Comebacks expanded

The show's writers gave Murphy Brown Snappy Comebacks that do more than simply reflect what the other characters say. Many of Murphy's responses expand our perception. They give us a perspective of the larger world. They are Inspired Observations.

In the next chapter, you'll discover Inspired Observations from masters including Harriet Tubman, Oscar Wilde, Mohandas Gandhi, Swiss novelist Max Frisch, Zsa Zsa Gabor, and the incomparable Yogi Berra.

CHAPTER 13

Inspired Observations

Inspired Observations are fresh views of the world that make us laugh with recognition or sigh with resignation.

Yogi Berra knew the key to an Inspired Observation.

"You can observe a lot," he said, "by just watching."

Observing oneself

Dorothy Parker, the mistress of the verbal hand grenade, could even toss one of those grenades at herself.

I like to have a martini,

Two at the very most.

After three I'm under the table.

After four I'm under my host.

Oscar Levant (1906–1972) was a brilliant American pianist, prolific composer, author, comedian, and actor. He was also famous for his morbid personality.

"I don't drink," Levant observed. "I don't like it. It makes me feel good."

Levant did not try to hide his neuroses and hypochondria. Toward the end of his life, his wife frequently committed him to mental hospitals. Levant once observed, "There's a fine line between genius and insanity. I have erased this line."

At a party one evening, Levant's friend George Gershwin needled his fellow composer. "Oscar," he asked, "why don't you play us a medley of your hit?"

Alexander Woollcott also could not resist a jab at Levant. "There isn't anything the matter with Levant that a few miracles wouldn't cure."

Woollcott (1887–1943), a member of the Algonquin Round Table, also observed himself. "Everything I like," he said, "is either illegal, immoral, or fattening."

George Bernard Shaw admitted his problems with women when he said, "The fickleness of the women I love is only equaled by the infernal constancy of the women who love me."

"The extraordinary thing about my mother," said George Gershwin, "she's so modest about me."

Zsa Zsa Gabor was married nine times. "I am a marvelous housekeeper," she said. "Every time I leave a man, I keep his house."

A cynic's observations of the world

Writer Ambrose Bierce observed himself as well as other people in his best-known work, *The Devil's Dictionary*, published in 1911.

Cynic, n. A blackguard whose faulty vision sees things as they are, not as they ought to be.

Acquaintance, n. A person whom we know well enough to borrow from, but not well enough to lend to. A degree of friendship called slight when its object is poor or obscure, and intimate when he is rich or famous.

Eccentricity, n. A method of distinction so cheap that fools employ it to accentuate their incapacity.

Then as today, the law and politics were easy targets.

Lawyer, n. One skilled in circumvention of the law.

Recount, n. In American politics, another throw of the dice, accorded to the player against whom they are loaded.

Bierce made no secret of his feelings about religion.

Religion, *n.* A daughter of Hope and Fear, explaining to Ignorance the nature of the Unknowable.

Pray, *v.* To ask that the laws of the universe be annulled in behalf of a single petitioner confessedly unworthy.

Clergyman, *n.* A man who undertakes the management of our spiritual affairs as a method of bettering his temporal ones.

Bierce never wrote about his personal life, but *The Devil's Dictionary* came out late in his career, so it probably contains elements of autobiography. In the summer of 1871, he met Mary Ellen "Mollie" Day, the daughter of a successful San Francisco mining family. A photograph shows a young woman with strong and beautiful features.

Bait, *n.* A preparation that renders the hook more palatable. The best kind is beauty.

On December 25, 1871 Miss Day and Mr. Bierce were married.

Bride, *n.* A woman with a fine prospect of happiness behind her.

Husband, *n.* One who, having dined, is charged with the care of the plate.

Communism vs. comedy

Karl Marx (1818–1883) was one of the fathers of Communism, a movement not noted for its humor. Groucho Marx was famous for making people laugh. Clearly, the two Marxes were not related.

When Groucho celebrated his seventy-first birthday in 1961, letters and telegrams of congratulation poured in. A wonderful observation came in a telegram from composer Irving Berlin.

"The world would not be in such a snarl,

had Marx been Groucho instead of Karl."

Mean observations

Margot Asquith (1864–1945) was the wife of Herbert Asquith, British Prime Minister from 1908 to 1916. Apparently she did not think much of her husband's successor, David Lloyd-George.

"Lloyd-George," she said, "couldn't see a belt without hitting below it."

Margot probably had a few flaws herself. The October 22, 1927 edition of *The New Yorker* contains an article about Asquith and her book *Lay Sermons*. The author of the article was our very own mistress of the verbal hand grenade, Dorothy Parker.

"No matter where she takes off from, she brings the discourse back to Margot Asquith."

"The affair between Margot Asquith and Margot Asquith will live as one of the prettiest love stories in all literature."

Observing voters and their cats

Before he ran for President against Dwight D. Eisenhower, Adlai Stevenson was the Governor of Illinois from 1949 to 1953. The state Senate passed Bill No. 93 (supported by bird lovers) declaring that cats were a public nuisance if they were wandering around unescorted by a human being. Stevenson vetoed the bill, with this comment to the public.

"It is in the nature of cats to do a certain amount of unescorted roaming. The problem of cat versus bird is as old as time. If we attempt to solve it by legislation who knows but what we may be called upon to take sides as well in the age-old problem of dog versus cat, bird versus bird, or even bird versus worm. In my opinion, the State of Illinois and its local governing bodies already have enough to do without trying to control feline delinquency. For these reasons, and not because I love birds the less or cats the more, I veto and withhold my approval from Senate Bill No. 93."

Slavery

Andrew Jackson, who owned hundreds of slaves, was the seventh President of the United States. In April 2016, the United States Department of the Treasury announced that Jackson's image on the front side of the $20 bill would be replaced by that of a woman who was born a slave.

One of the bravest Americans ever, Harriet Tubman was born in Maryland in about 1822. She escaped to the North in 1849, but quickly returned to Maryland to rescue her family. Tubman returned thirteen times to bring slaves to freedom. Slave owners posted rewards for her capture. It is not pleasant to think what would have happened to her if she had been captured.

Although she personally led about seventy people to freedom, she was an essential part of a larger movement called the Underground Railway, an informal alliance of people who helped countless more slaves escape.

Tubman probably did not exaggerate when she said, "I freed a thousand slaves. I could have freed a thousand more if only they knew they were slaves."

Gandhi said, "The moment the slave resolves that he will no longer be a slave, his fetters fall. He frees himself and shows the way to others. Freedom and slavery are mental states."

Tubman's and Gandhi's words resonate powerfully today, when we willingly use smart phones and wearable technology to gradually enslave ourselves to corporations and government. The result is erosion of our privacy, and even physical risk.

Slavery to technology

On December 25, 2015 a man from the Midwest was walking along the top of the Sunset Cliffs in San Diego, California. With his attention entirely on his smart phone, he was in the virtual world, not the physical one. As a result, he walked over the edge of the cliff and fell sixty feet to his death. He was thirty-three, the father of one.

Some fifty-eight years before this tragedy, Swiss playwright and novelist Max Frisch (1911–1991) observed the patterns of behavior that would eventually result in texting while driving, as well as walking off a cliff while staring at a hand-held device. His 1957 novel *Homo Faber* describes technology as "... the knack of arranging the world so that we need not experience it."

Technology continued (television)

"I find television very educating," said Groucho Marx.

"Every time somebody turns on the set, I go into the other room and read a book."

The much praised, much maligned cigar

One critic, probably Horace Greeley (1811–1872), observed that "A cigar has a fire at one end and a fool at the other."

Someone else provided a slightly different perspective.

"I kissed my first girl and smoked my first cigarette on the same day," said conductor Arturo Toscanini. "I haven't had time for tobacco since."

Novelist Aldous Huxley had plenty of time for tobacco.

"You should hurry up and acquire the cigar habit," he wrote. "It's one of the major happinesses. And so much more lasting than love, so much less costly in emotional wear and tear."

"The most futile and disastrous day seems well spent when

it is reviewed through the blue, fragrant smoke of a Havana cigar," wrote Evelyn Waugh.

According to George Burns, cigars have another advantage. "If I had taken my doctor's advice and quit smoking when he advised me to," Burns said at age 98, "I wouldn't have lived to go to his funeral."

Winston Churchill loved cigars and may well have smoked more of them than anyone else on earth. At Chartwell Manor, his country home in Kent, he stocked between 3,000 and 4,000 cigars in a room next to his study. Sir Stafford Cripps seemed to have only one slight pleasure, an occasional cigar. Cripps (1889–1952) was Churchill's exact opposite in other ways as well. Where Churchill bubbled with humor, Cripps was dour.

Churchill inspired millions of people with his speeches. Cripps was a boring speaker. During World War II, Churchill frequently appeared in public with a large cigar; Cripps announced he himself had given up cigars as a symbolic sacrifice.

"Too bad," commented Churchill when he heard the news. "It was his last contact with humanity."

When Churchill visited North Africa during the war, he surveyed the bleak desert landscape. "Here we are," he observed, "marooned in all these miles of sand—not one blade of grass or drop of water or a flower. How Cripps would love it."

Oscar Wilde's observation of America

"America had often been discovered before Columbus," said Wilde, "but it had always been hushed up."

During Wilde's 1882 tour of America, he went to California, where he met some very rough men, including gold miners. One evening, drinking with these fellows in a saloon, he noticed a sign on the wall.

PLEASE DON'T SHOOT THE PIANIST. HE IS DOING HIS BEST.

Said Wilde, "This sign is the only rational method of art criticism I have ever come across."

More impressive to the miners than Wilde's appreciation of art criticism was his tremendous capacity for alcohol. Trying to match him drink for drink, the miners literally ended up under the table.

The Duke of Windsor's observation of America

In 1955 and again in 1970, the Duke of Windsor visited America. A March 5, 1957 article in *Look* magazine quoted the Duke as saying, "The thing that impresses me most about America is the way parents obey their children."

The Duke (1894–1972) was formerly King Edward VIII of England. When he realized that British custom would not allow him to marry the woman he loved, the twice-divorced American Wallis Simpson, Edward abdicated the throne in 1936 and became the Duke of Windsor. This act might have been the greatest thing he did for his country.

In those days just before World War II, he and Wallis were outspoken admirers of Adolph Hitler.

Adolph Hitler's observation of the Duke of Windsor

Hitler said, "I am certain through him permanent friendly relations could have been achieved [between Germany and England]. If he had stayed, everything would have been different. His abdication was a severe loss for us."

Churchill's observation of Hitler

In 1941, Churchill said to his personal secretary, John Colville, "If Hitler invaded Hell, I would make at least a favourable reference to the devil in the House of Commons."

The next day, June 22, Germany invaded the Soviet Union.

More Inspired Observations

In May 1961, President and Mrs. Kennedy went to Paris. Jacqueline Kennedy spoke French fluently, and she charmed the French people even more than her charismatic husband did. Kennedy gracefully acknowledged the fact as he began a speech. "I do not think it altogether inappropriate to introduce myself," he said. "I am the man who accompanied Jacqueline Kennedy to Paris, and I have enjoyed it."

Kennedy also enjoyed being President. "The pay is good," he said, "and I can walk to work."

With his dry New England wit, Calvin Coolidge made plenty of Inspired Observations.

In 1929, nearing the end of his term as President, he said, "Perhaps one of the most important accomplishments of my administration has been minding my own business."

Coolidge also said, "Nothing is easier than spending the public money. It does not appear to belong to anybody."

Larry's observations

At first, I didn't want to put my own observations in a chapter named "Inspired Observations." I thought it would be inappropriate for such a modest person.

But I am very proud of my modesty, so here they are.

LARRY'S LAWS OF THE UNIVERSE

1. Things come in clumps.

> Galaxies, grapes, and airborne emergencies. If you're flying an airplane and the engine starts to cough and sputter, you'll immediately hit turbulence, your radio will cease to function, and your passenger will throw up on you. Other things that come in clumps include customers, problems with the IRS, girlfriends, boyfriends, clients, project problems, money....

2. Any given mess will expand to fit the space allotted for it.

> A small desk has a small mess, and most people's garages are filled with stuff that's not good enough to keep, but too good to throw away. As this mess expands, it pushes the expensive automobiles outside.

3. The fact that something cannot be proven does not necessarily mean it is true.

> Astrology and past lives come to mind.

4. If you improve something enough, you will ruin it.

> Any product labeled "New and Improved." Tools with plastic where metal used to be. The latest software upgrade.

5. Reality is an illusion.

> What we call "reality" is what we perceive through our senses. But our senses are really just a collection of nerve impulses that filter and interpret the world. That's as illusory as it gets.

6. All illusions are real.

> Like reality, illusions are just a collection of nerve impulses. That's as real as it gets.

7. If you live long enough, something will kill you.

> This Law of the Universe exists mostly to cheer people up.

8. Invention is the mother of necessity.

> I never needed a cell phone until cell phones were invented.

9. Many opportunities are invisible at first.

> If someone criticizes you for having a new tool belt, and you have no Snappy Comeback, you will eventually write a book.

10. An alternative to the Snappy Comeback actually exists.

> It's amazing how simple it is.

CHAPTER 14

An Alternative to the Snappy Comeback

The 1950 film *Harvey* starring James Stewart contains a perfect alternative to the Snappy Comeback.

Stewart's character, Elwood P. Dowd, says:

"Years ago my mother used to say to me, she'd say, 'In this world, Elwood, you must be (she always called me Elwood). In this world, Elwood, you must be oh so smart or oh so pleasant.' Well, for years I was smart.

"I recommend pleasant. You may quote me."

I just did, Elwood, and I thank you.

I also have other people to thank, non-fictional people who are both smart **and** pleasant.

Acknowledgements

When I was wondering if this book was even worth beginning, my brother, Brian Lansburgh, assured me it was. Over the course of the project, his encouragement has been constant and his comments astute. He also said, "Be sure to include lots of pictures."

Fritz Kasten's Inspired Observations on the overall structure of the manuscript opened my eyes. His comments on its strong points and its flaws were encouraging and absolutely essential.

Gayle Crowder's omnivision is amazing. She reviewed the work as a whole, and simultaneously used her uncanny ability to spot the tiniest typos. Any typos you spot are ones I added after Gayle went over the manuscript.

Craig Steiger kept up a constant stream of source materials coming my way in the form of books actually printed on paper.

When I reviewed the manuscript of Margaret Simeone's wonderful book *Avery and Me*, I gained insights about the power of self-awareness, expectation, and trust. Those insights helped me write this book.

While I am writing, I go into a trance. My wife, Sarah, helped the project with ongoing good humor and patience for her zombie-like husband. She also read the manuscript and found some mistakes that would have embarrassed me if they had appeared in the book.

My thanks also go to all the people whom I have quoted. Their words have expanded my view of the world and given me lots of laughs.

And, of course, I thank the guy who criticized me for having a new tool belt.

Select Bibliography

Bierce, Ambrose, *The Devil's Dictionary*, Introduction by Angus Calder
Bloomsbury New York and London
>First published in 1911, this book's cynical observations still ring true, and still make us laugh.

Chandler, Charlotte, *Hello, I Must Be Going: Groucho and His Friends*
Simon and Schuster Paperbacks
>The late Charlotte Chandler was not only Groucho's biographer. She was also his friend. The book features many fascinating conversation with Groucho.

Lansburgh, Brian
Brian's Coast Guard Story: www.tailwheelersjournal.com
Article #146 *The Winged S Award*
>This web site focuses on aviation essentials. But even if you're not a pilot, you'll love the writing.

Manchester, William, *The Last Lion: Winston Spencer Churchill: Visions of Glory, 1874-1932* (Volume 1)
Boston: Little, Brown & Co.

Manchester, William, *The Last Lion: Winston Spencer Churchill: Alone, 1932-1940* (Volume 2)
Boston: Little, Brown & Co.

Manchester, William and Reid, Paul, *The Last Lion: Winston Spencer Churchill: Defender of the Realm, 1940-1965* (Volume 3)
Boston: Little, Brown & Co.
>These three volumes are simply the best biographies of Churchill ever written. They give you an extremely close look at Churchill the man, and they provide a vivid portrait of the world in which he lived. William Manchester died while writing Volume 3. Paul Reid has done a brilliant job of completing the work.

Morris, Roy Jr.: *Ambrose Bierce: Alone in Bad Company*
Crown Publishers, Inc.
> Like Manchester, Morris has the rare ability to bring historical characters and their times into vivid reality.

Wilde, Oscar, *The Importance of Being Earnest*
> More than a hundred years after its first performance, Wilde's play is still a delight to read.

Made in the USA
San Bernardino, CA
10 June 2018